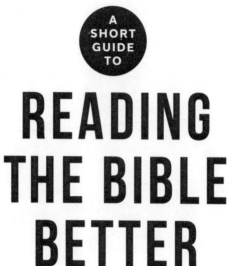

A SHORT GUIDE TO

READING THE BIBLE BETTER

A
SHORT
GUIDE
TO

READING THE BIBLE BETTER

GEORGE H. GUTHRIE

PUBLISHING
NASHVILLE, TENNESSEE

Published by B&H Publishing Group
Nashville, Tennessee

Dewey Decimal Classification: 220.07
Subject Heading: BIBLE—READING / BOOKS AND READING

Cover design by B&H Publishing Group.
Illustrations by Kristi Smith, Juicebox Designs.

1 2 3 4 5 6 • 26 25 24 23 22

To David and Jill Shanks
with deep appreciation for
your partnership in this work

Contents

CHAPTER 1

An Invitation to Reading the Bible Better

Dear Bibliophilos,[1] words are more powerful than
a nuclear bomb, for words move the world!

THIS IS A BOOK ABOUT WORDS. Words have already shaped your life
a great deal, putting things in motion, setting trajectories for
your relationships, work, interests, commitments, and hopes.
Words have hurt or healed you, delighted or devastated you,
instructed and informed you. In short, words have played a
large role in defining who you are today.

A word-rich, life-defining moment came for the British
people during WWII, in a span of dark days stretching from
May 26 to June 4, 1940. The British Expeditionary Force
had been sent to stop the advance of the Nazis, who were

pushing through the Netherlands like a wildfire and were now threatening to overrun Belgium and France. But the Germans executed a brilliant "pincer" movement, hemming in and pushing the British troops and their allies to the beaches of the small Belgian town of Dunkirk. Some 350,000 Allied soldiers were threatened with annihilation. Word reached the British people of this threat and they prayed earnestly, lifting words to heaven as they anxiously waited.

Then, ringing out from the dark pall that hung over the world in that moment, the trapped troops sent back to England a brief message of three little words: ". . . and if not." The British, who at that time in history were more biblically aware than we are today, recognized the words immediately as taken from the story of Shadrach, Meshach, and Abednego in Daniel 3. These three Jewish exiles had been taken from their homeland and placed under King Nebuchadnezzar's rule. When he told them to worship a gold statue he built, the men put their trust in God despite the known result of their defiance: being thrown into a fiery furnace. As they were told their fate and the furnace was heated seven times hotter than normal, their words confidently rang out: *Our God can rescue us from your hand, but even if he doesn't, we won't serve your gods.* Words coming out of Dunkirk in effect said, "We trust God to deliver us, but even if he does not, we will not bow to the forces of evil!"

In this darkest point of the conflict, the German army suddenly received a halt order, pausing their advance to consolidate their troops. The three-day pause opened a window of opportunity for the British and their allies. Those simple, powerful words, "and if not," helped galvanize the nation and put into motion what has been called, "the miracle of Dunkirk." Word went out along the coast of England. Boats were needed to mount a rescue mission. Hurriedly, more than 800 vessels—boats of every shape, size, and purpose—were assembled into a ragtag fleet of rescue. Over the next eight days of evacuation, 338,226 troops were saved.

Think of the power of those three little words, "and if not"—two conjunctions and a negative. They are unassuming words, used countless times a day by everyone from little children just learning to speak to the most eloquent adult. Yet, in the right place, at the right time, those words were *powerful*, mobilizing a nation. Those words were courageous, communicating a passionate resolve to not give up in the face of devastating loss. Those words were *almost playful*, evoking a very old, very good story. And those words were *biblical*, embraced as God's Word, shouted boldly into a moment of overwhelming need, both in Babylon and at Dunkirk. Three little words put the moment in motion and in focus.

THE POWER OF WORDS

Each of us who live in North America pour approximately 16,000 words into the world every day, some 860.3 million words in a lifetime! Levi Lusko tells us that there are seventy-two different muscles in our bodies that have to work in unison to shape our words.[2] So we might well ask: What are you and I doing with all of those words, so masterfully shaped, which we are sending into the world? The answer is simple: we are moving the world.

Just as with Dunkirk, words put things in motion. Words carry impact, whether it's small as an answer to a friend's simple question, or life-altering, as when a bride says, "I do" or an employer says, "You've got the job!"—or "You're fired!" Words can heal a heart, but they can also wield a wicked cut, as when a teacher says, "You are an idiot," or a stranger hurls an insult, or a "friend" slanders us. Nathaniel Hawthorne once wrote:

> Words—so innocent and powerless as they
> are, as standing in a dictionary, how potent
> for good and evil they become in the hands
> of one who knows how to combine them.[3]

What we intuitively long for, of course, is the "potent for good" side of that equation. We love to receive kind, helpful, encouraging, or beautiful words, and most of us really do want to do better with speaking life-giving, life-building, life-affirming words to others.

But no one—no one—knows how to wield words for good like God! *God spoke*, and the foundations of all that we know as reality came into existence: "By faith we understand that the universe was created by the word of God, so that what is seen was made from things that are not visible" (Heb. 11:3). Genesis tells us that *God spoke* light and darkness; the heavens and planet earth, sun, moon, and stars; the vast reaches of the universe. *God spoke*, and the beauty of the grandest mountains, the life-giving waters of the earth's great rivers, and the glorious plethora of flora and fauna painted across vast landscapes came into existence. Animals of every shape and size started moving. We as human beings were born and given great things to do. Then, *God spoke* a blessing over that creation and declared it to be good. In light of such creative eloquence, we might say that words lie at the heart of the universe, foundational for life itself. God is a communicator, and if God spoke all that we know into existence, it means that communication itself is behind the universe. Think of that. *Communication is behind the universe.* Words are so much more than mere human invention, some natural product of being in the world.

God spoke, and the foundations of all that we know as reality came into existence.

Significantly, Jesus's life and ministry bear this out. Jesus himself is called "the Word": "In the beginning was the Word, and the Word was with God, and the Word was God" (John 1:1). Jesus, "the Word," put much in motion in the world through powerful words, whether proclaiming the coming of the kingdom (Mark 1:15), calming a storm (Mark 4:35–41), healing (Luke 7:2–10), or shaping lives through powerful teaching (Matt. 5–7). Moreover, Jesus himself pointed us to the authority of Scripture (Matt. 5:17–18), making clear that Scripture is the Word of God written for the people of God so they might know him and live out his mission in the world.

A VISION FOR READING THE BIBLE BETTER

You and I need to embrace the powerful, beautiful, life-giving words of God on a regular basis. Various surveys in different cultures, over the past half century, have determined that the number one predictor of a person's spiritual health is the regular practice of personal Bible reading. Nothing else comes close. Based on what we said above, this simply makes sense. If God has designed all of life, if his words form the creative foundation for everything, then his words would be a key to life in this world that he has created. Further, if we are made in his image and for relationship with him, then, as with any relationship worth having, communication is vital. If our purpose in life is to live for him and to his glory, and the Scriptures shape us for his mission, then God's Word provides us with a means to that very desirable end.

Most basically, as we thrive in the Word of God, knowing and living the Scriptures, we have the opportunity to walk with the God of the universe, to know him and be shaped by him. This is our purpose. The Scriptures play a vital role in us fulfilling our purpose in the world. Consequently, *there is no more important task in life than hearing from God and trusting him on the basis of his Word.* I mean that quite literally: *no more important task.* Everything else in our lives is shaped by whether or not we are living out of a life grounded in the Word of God, the Bible. We need to read it and read it better than we ever have before, so that we can live it well.

As we thrive in the Word of God, knowing and living the Scriptures, we have the opportunity to walk with the God of the universe.

So you are invited to walk with me as we figure out how to read better this amazing book we call "the Bible." Perhaps you have tried reading the Bible before and the experience wasn't that great. I am here to help. A wise person once said, "If you have a dull axe and don't sharpen it, using it will wear you out!"[4] If you want to read the Bible in a way that will give you life rather than exhaust you, sharpen your skills. Like anything worth doing, reading the Bible takes time and effort to learn to do well.

There is no more important task in life than hearing from God and trusting him on the basis of his Word.

Over the next five chapters we'll discuss:

1. motivation and spiritual condition as foundational for reading Scripture
2. how to understand the messages of Scripture
3. how to read the Bible in community with others
4. how to read for personal transformation

5. how to enter the grand story of Scripture

6. and how to access great tools for better Bible reading

But first, we need to talk about the single most important factor keeping most of us from enjoying our experience of the Bible.

DISCUSS

1. Have there been times in your life when a single word changed your course?

2. How have you been shaped by the words spoken to you? Spoken about you?

3. If hearing from God and trusting him on the basis of his Word is our most important task, what steps do you need to take to make this more central in your life? What questions or learning should you pursue?

4. How have you felt worn out reading God's Word in the past? What are your hopes in reading this book for sharpening your skills in this area?

PRACTICE

1. The first step in fruitful Bible reading is consistency. What time each day will you commit to reading God's Word? How will you set up accountability measures to ensure you are engaging consistently?

2. As you read, take note of specific words, investigating the text thoroughly by asking questions and making observations.

3. Discuss what you are reading with others who are committed to reading God's Word well.

CHAPTER 2

Look to the Heart

*Dear Bibliophilos, in Bible reading, you must above
all get to the heart of the matter!*

A LITTLE OVER TWO decades ago, my wife and I bought a piece of
property in the country. It had been a dream, really, that we
might be able to choose a beautiful plot of land and develop
it into a homeplace. There we would raise our children, who
were just seven and four years of age at the time. The property,
which we named "Shepherd's Way," had belonged to a Mr.
Johnson, who had moved to this part of Tennessee as a nine-
year-old in 1923, rolling up to this small and beautiful piece of
earth in a wagon. We planned a spot for the house just behind
a pond, at the end of what would become a long driveway

cutting past very large, old oak trees. Eventually, the work began and was finished, and our dream became a reality. It was a memory-filled gift to us and our children for two decades.

One of our first tasks for this new home was to have a well dug. Running under our property, 125 feet below the surface, was one of the best aquifers in North America, a source of sweet, cold, clear water that would keep our family and our land hydrated for years. Fortunately, a near neighbor was one of the best well-drilling professionals in the county. At about retirement age, he not only installed our well but serviced it long after formally leaving the business, normally asking for no more payment than one of Pat's wonderful pies. But on one occasion, the motor—the "heart" of the whole operation and the key to tapping into that precious source of water—went out, and we needed a more extensive, expensive fix, having lost the power to get the water to the surface.

THE HEART AS THE KEY

If you are a committed Christian, you probably have had moments in life in which you have said to yourself, "I need to read the Bible more!" You may have thought about the endeavor in terms of "When will I do it?," "What plan should I use?," and "What do I need to do?" Certainly, reading the Bible needs to be approached with such questions, but I want to suggest in this chapter that the *key* to reading the Bible well, in a rhythm of life that thrums with interest and leads to real transformation, lies below the surface of such questions, much deeper, in the regions of the heart.

The key to reading the Bible well lies in the regions of the heart.

In a sense, the powerful, eternal Word of the living God is like that aquifer running under our house in the country, always there, a resource of life and refreshment and nourishment. In fact, Psalm 1 uses the word picture of a constantly running stream to describe the experience of a "blessed" person who delights in God's Word: "He is like a tree planted beside flowing streams" (Ps. 1:3). Yet, our hearts, like the well motor nestled deep in the earth under our house, must be in good condition to tap the Word in ways that lead to life and change. With a well, if the motor is broken, water simply will not come to the surface. We can have the pipes in place and nice faucets for delivery. We may have a timer that sets a rhythm for watering the lawn. Yet, if the motor is broken, there is no life-sustaining water.

Similarly, if our hearts are not in the right posture, open and made pliable and receptive by the Holy Spirit, reading the Bible will not be the intended life-sustaining delight. It will fall flat. We can have a nice Bible, a time for Bible reading, a place for our reading, and even a sense of resolve that "this time I am going to stick with it!" Nevertheless, our "practice of Bible reading," no matter how well-intentioned, will not last if our hearts are not addressed first.

MOTIVATIONS AND THE CONDITION OF THE HEART

The Bible stresses that we must give attention to the motivations and the condition of our hearts. Proverbs 4:23 reads: "Guard your heart above all else, for it is the source of life." In the remainder of this chapter, I want to talk about how we might guard our hearts, that is, how we might give attention to what is going on with our hearts. I want us to think about what motivates us in life.

What really moves us to act? To what do we want to give time and why? Our motivations reflect the condition of our hearts. Is our heart healthy spiritually? Is our heart in a place and posture to hear what God is saying to us?

Our motivations reflect the
condition of our hearts.

Specifically in terms of reading God's Word, our motivations affect what might move our hearts to commit time to God's Word. Do we value what the Word has to offer us? Our spiritual "heart condition" influences our heart's ability to hear and act on God's Word. Our spiritual condition can facilitate or severely restrict the impact of God's Word on our lives. In some ways, the condition of our hearts lies at the very bedrock of a life built on God's Word. In turn, as we begin to address the condition of our hearts and begin embracing the Word, the Word will further shape the condition of our hearts to be even more receptive, shaping our motivations in good directions. In that sense, the heart is both the source and the goal of our Bible reading.

Valuing the Good Gifts of God's Word

In reality, our motivations point to what we value most in life. What do we value? Why do we value the things that we hold most dear? When we speak of motivations, then, we address what we value and our drive to go after what we value.

Whether we realize it or not, God's words are far more valuable than we can imagine, far more valuable than the biggest bank account or our most earnestly desired possessions: "They are more desirable than gold—than an abundance of pure gold" (Ps. 19:10). If we could see the Bible for what it is— communication from the living God himself—we would be driven to it like a man dying of thirst is driven to water. So, in terms of motivation, we need to hear and grasp the astounding ways in which the Bible adds great value to our lives. Far from mere self-help foolery, the Bible itself celebrates the value of God's Word in an artful array of colorful word pictures. We could celebrate many of these as strong motivations for reading it, but let's consider four—the lamp, sword, rock, and honey.

Lamp: Our Need for Guidance

One of the most beautiful verses in the Bible reads: "Your word is a lamp for my feet and a light on my path" (Ps. 119:105). In the Old Testament era, lamps were made of fired clay, formed by making a shallow saucer which was pinched on one side to manage the wick, which normally was made of flax. Olive oil served as the fuel. Normally such lamps were used indoors, but the image here evokes a walk at night along a path. Imagine an old farmer walking through a field, tending to his sheep. The path is uneven, studded with rocks and pocked with holes. The path winds along the edge of a drop-off and is perilous. The light shows him both where he should step, alerting him to what is ahead, and where he must not step, lest he fall into serious trouble.

The image is immediately transferable to many situations in the modern world. We use night-lights to guide us when making our way to a bathroom in the middle of the night. We use flashlights to retrieve something from the backyard, or a basement, or a dark closet. The light guides our steps by illuminating dark corners and uncertain footing. If you ever camp, you probably have had the experience of making your way down a dark path at night to collect firewood. The light shows you what is ahead and, perhaps, keeps wild animals away!

And this image of the lamp speaks powerfully and figuratively to where we often find ourselves in this very dark world. You may ask: Where and how can I "walk" through this difficult situation at work, or that relationship with a family member, or an unsettling reality in the culture at large? In a world of social unrest and pandemics and pressures, what *should* I do? What should I *not* do? We need guidance. We need a perspective bigger than our own to help us make right decisions. So, as a key motivation, *we should long to read God's Word to get answers for life, to know how we should live and respond to the world around us.*

When we say that the Bible is like a lamp that guides us, we do not mean, of course, that it gives specific direction on which TV to buy, or which person to date, or where to go on vacation. Rather, God's good Word guides us in terms of *key patterns* in life, *principles* by which we should live, and *practices* that we should embrace. In short, the Bible trains us to live well, in God's ways, both to shape the directions of our lives and to guard us from falling into things that might do us harm. As we read the Bible daily, we learn to think about life the way that God wants us to think; this shapes the decisions that we make and the impact that we have on others in the world.

The Bible trains us to live well, in God's ways, both to shape the directions of our lives and to guard us from falling into things that might do us harm.

Sword: The Bible Corrects Us

Recently, my youngest brother, Al, had surgery. There was a growing tumor on one of his kidneys, and the doctors thought it might be malignant. They waited for months before taking it out (which made us all a bit nervous), saying that the spot needed to get to a certain size before it could be removed and assessed. Yet, the day came for the surgery. The highly trained surgeon cut strategically into my brother's body and cut away part of the kidney. The process was painful, with care needed during recovery, but it was successful, and the months of distress and discomfort gave way to real thanks and hope for the future. The cut was the cure.

Hebrews 4:12–13 says:

> For the word of God is living and effective and sharper than any double-edged sword, penetrating as far as the separation of soul and spirit, joints and marrow. It is able to judge the thoughts and intentions of the heart. No creature is hidden from him, but all things are naked and exposed to the eyes of him to whom we must give an account.

In his commentary on Hebrews, Harold Attridge calls this passage "a rhapsody on God's penetrating word."[1] Here, too, we see that the cut is the cure.

In Hebrews 4:12 the author may have in mind a Roman *gladius*, a short sword about twenty inches long. The *gladius* had a sharp edge down both sides to cut both ways in close hand-to-hand combat. But the key to the image here, as Attridge notes, is penetration. The author of Hebrews presents God's Word as "living," a powerful force in the world—far more than just words on a page—a sharp word of discernment which actively penetrates the darkest corners of the human heart. It is "effective" in that it has the ability to bring about results, reaching down into our innermost being, the place of "soul and spirit, joints and marrow," judging "the thoughts and intentions of the heart." Like a surgeon wielding a scalpel to cut out the motivations, sins, and attitudes that can hurt us and others, God's Word cuts to cure. God's Word has the uncanny ability to *correct us at the deepest, darkest levels of our thoughts and motivations.*

As with my brother's surgery, the spiritual correction of God's Word may be painful, but it is a really good gift. For things grow inside of us that can cause great damage to our spiritual health if not addressed. And the dark corners of our hearts will be addressed, now or later—"all things are naked and exposed to the eyes of him to whom we must give an account." So we should be motivated to read the Bible because it addresses things that need to be addressed in our lives. It corrects us in ways that we need to be corrected.

Rock: The Bible Gives Us Stability

When we were young, my grandad built a tree house for me and my brothers in his spacious yard in Tennessee. Along the edge of the yard there were trees reaching to the sky, their branches transforming right before our eyes to pirate ships, an island hideaway, or a fort. About ten feet in the air, the sides of the tree house were attached to a small group of trees, forming a rectangle, and the floor was made of pine planks. We were so excited! At our first opportunity, we climbed the ladder to check it out. One surprise was that a long plank stuck out one side of the structure. We thought, "We have a gangplank, just like on a pirate ship!" What we did not realize is that grandad had not yet finished the tree house, and the jutting plank was a board that had not been nailed down! Needless to say, when my brother David stepped out onto that plank—I graciously allowed him to go first—our dreams of the pirate ship came crashing down, as did David.

I don't need to tell you that we live in an unstable world. In recent years we have seen pandemics, wide-ranging social unrest, too many acts of random violence, and political conflict across the world. Depending on where you live, you may have been threatened by tornadoes, hurricanes, wildfires, or earthquakes. You may live under the threat of persecution from political or religious extremists, and you may feel dismayed by the dramatically changing values in the culture in which you live. In your personal life, you may have faced financial uncertainty, major health crises, the dissolving of relationships with family members or those who were once friends, or just the day-to-day pressures of work. All of the above can lead to feelings of emotional vulnerability or instability. It is hard to walk where the "boards" of life are not nailed down, where there is no stability.

Yet here we find another great gift in God's Word and a corresponding motivation to read it on a regular basis. In Matthew 7:24–27 Jesus said:

> "Therefore, everyone who hears these words of mine and acts on them will be like a wise man who built his house on the rock. The rain fell, the rivers rose, and the winds blew and pounded that house. Yet it didn't collapse, because its foundation was on the rock. But everyone who hears these words of mine

and doesn't act on them will be like a foolish man who built his house on the sand. The rain fell, the rivers rose, the winds blew and pounded that house, and it collapsed. It collapsed with a great crash."

In the modern world we often lay a foundation when building a house. When Pat and I built our house in Tennessee, we first had a "footing," a trench of concrete put down where all of the supporting walls of the house would be. This gave the house stability, so that the walls would not shift or move with time and tremors. In the ancient world, builders—remember that Jesus and his father Joseph were builders—dug down in the earth to find a rock, or they at times would put large rocks or blocks down, to provide a stable foundation for a house.

Jesus said that his words are like a rock under a house assaulted by a violent climate, rain, wind, and rivers pounding relentlessly. Do you ever feel like that in life? Like you are being pounded by forces in the world, whether global or local, social or personal? I do. Jesus said that when we hear and act on his words, those words give us stability in such a world, and that is an amazing gift. God's Word gives us a sense of place in the world as God's people and a confidence in the face of massive uncertainties, because he is with us, and he is not surprised by the challenges. He speaks to us words of perspective and comfort and hope.

At the end of my time in university and just after, I went through a season of clinical depression—though I did not know to call it that at the time. The deep emotional and spiritual darkness is hard to describe to others, but it grew in part out of the question: "Why do I believe the things I say I believe?" I sought counsel from others, but the key for my recovery was being driven to God's Word as a rock of stability, a lifeline of hope, and an anchor that holds in the great storms of life. I have found the Word to be that rock, and over the past forty years, it has continued to be a rock of stability for me through many storms of life. The stability given by the Word should motivate us to read it consistently.

Honey: The Bible Delights Us

Finally, we should read the Bible because it is first and foremost a delight—a delight ultimately because it leads us to know the God of the universe himself. Intimacy grows in the context of communication. Through God's Word, we meet with God. Through the pages of Scripture, we learn to know and love the God we serve, and it is a joy to know him and be known by him! When was the last time you had pure *joy* in reading some portion of the Bible? When was the last time you heard God speak to you in the pages of the Bible, and those words moved you like sweet words spoken to you by a cherished friend? Psalm 119:103 reads: "How sweet your word is to my taste—sweeter than honey in my mouth." The word for *honey* in this verse is *dĕbaš*, a term that could be used either for honey from bees or the syrup from fruit like grapes or dates. In biblical times there was no sugar, so these were the sweet foods that people could eat. The image in the psalm is one of delight.

My wife, Pat, is a phenomenal cook. When our daughter Anna was finishing her university degree in graphic design, she decided to do a "legacy cookbook" for her senior project. Working with the rest of us in the family, she chose thirty of Pat's family recipes to include in the book, which she would design and publish. There would be breakfast foods, main dishes, breads, soups, and desserts. In the Spring of 2018, over a period of just six weeks, Pat cooked those recipes,

Anna staged and photographed the dishes, and I ate them. I also wrote introductory paragraphs describing where we got the recipe or how the dish fit into our family traditions, and our son, Joshua, typed in the recipes and organized the list of those in our broader networks who wanted a copy. Anna desktop-published the cookbook, pulling the whole together in a beautiful, professional volume. It was a big success.

The book is *beautiful*. The pictures of the food are pleasing to the eye. But the delight comes in the *tasting of the actual dishes as a family*! Pat's cinnamon rolls. Night-before French toast. Chicken potpie. Cheeseburger soup. Sweet potato stew. Pat's scones. The "hits" just keep on coming. My mouth is watering as I write these words! Yet, this book doesn't just reveal some of Pat's best recipes, it is a window into who Pat is and who we are as a family. Pat is hospitable and kind, and she loves to cook to show her love to others. Her recipes reveal her character. Meals are an important part of our family memories. Feasts and family go together. We delight in food around the table because we delight in each other.

As I have studied the Bible, I have been struck time and again with its artistic beauty, the words sweetening the reading at times, like the touch of a cinnamon roll to my lips.

For instance, the moment when Joseph reveals himself to his brothers, who look at him in stunned, terrified silence, almost always makes me laugh and cry at the same time (Gen. 45:1–3). The power and beauty of Jesus calming the storm (Mark 4:35–41), which also playfully echoes Psalm 107:29–30, where *God* stills the storm, is stunning. It leads us to ask with the disciples: "Who then is this?" The literary symmetry of the "Christ hymn" in Philippians 2:5–11 is so intricately crafted it rings in the ear like the finest poetry, if we only slow down to hear it. These delightful moments in Scripture reveal the heart of a God who is in control of all of our comings and goings, is powerful over anything we face, and is beautiful beyond compare. The sweetness of God's Word is found in its joy-*full* revelation of the Author.

The sweetness of God's Word is found in its joy-full revelation of the Author.

In our world, which can be so very dark and challenging and tedious, *we need beauty in which to find delight and, thus, hope.* One of the most poignant moments in J. R. R. Tolkien's *Lord of the Rings* trilogy comes as Frodo and Sam are struggling through a blasted wasteland on their way to Mordor, the mountain of doom; the smoke and stink of Sauron cover land and sky. In reading this part of the story, we feel the ever-increasing weight of the ring around Frodo's neck; we thirst with Sam for a cool, clean drink of water; and we especially struggle under the oppression of a seemingly overwhelming darkness that crushes and twists Middle Earth into a stingy, ugly thing. Then, Sam looks up.

> There, peeping among the cloud-wrack above a dark tor high up in the mountains, Sam saw a white star twinkle for a while. The beauty of it smote his heart, as he looked up out of the forsaken land, and hope returned to him. For like a shaft, clear and cold, the thought pierced him that in the end the Shadow was only a small and passing thing: there was light and high beauty forever beyond its reach. . . . Now, for a moment, his own fate, and even his master's, ceased to trouble him. He

crawled back into the brambles and laid himself by Frodo's side, and putting away all fear
he cast himself into a deep untroubled sleep.[2]

You and I need moments in which God's Word smites
our hearts with its beauty, igniting delight and awe and hope
in us. We need the Word to raise our heads above the reek of
day-to-day challenges to remind us that at the end of the day,
the darkness is "only a small and passing thing." There is light
and high beauty to be found in God's character, God's world,
and God's Word. We should be motivated to read God's Word
on a regular basis to see such beauty. We should be motivated
to read God's Word on a regular basis to know the Source of
beauty.

Friend, the Word of God has so much to offer us: guidance, correction, stability, and delight—and so much more.
But we will not know it unless we read it. So we should consider these motivations as drawing us to the Word.

The Condition of My Heart

As we move toward the end of this chapter on the heart,
we have one final, creative image, used in the Bible which we

need to consider. The word picture of the "seed and soils," found in Jesus's parable of the sower (Mark 4:1–20), is unique among the images we have looked at thus far. Whereas the lamp, the sword, the rock, and honey point to various benefits of God's Word, the image of the seed and soil uniquely points to the condition of the heart itself—taking us straight to the "heart" of the matter when it comes to reading God's Word. This parable is uniquely important, because Jesus himself said that if his disciples were not able to "get" or "understand" this parable, they would not be able to understand *any* of the other parables (4:13). Unless you understand and live out what it means to be "good soil," God's Word will not be fruitful in your life. In other words, this parable holds the key to hearing God's Word.

Unless you understand and live out what it means to be "good soil," God's Word will not be fruitful in your life.

In the parable of the sower, Jesus tells of a farmer sowing seeds in a field. In the land of Israel during Jesus's day, the farmer would carry a bag of seeds, probably strapped over his shoulder. Reaching into the bag, time and time again, he grabbed a handful of seeds and broadcast them over the ground, which was not yet tilled up. Once the seeds were spread over the field, he then turned the soil with a plough, covering the seeds in the process. If you have ever broadcast seeds over a lawn or garden, you know this is not an exact process. You can cast seeds up to the edge of the field, and some will blow over into the area beyond that edge; and this is exactly the situation described in the parable. In fact, in Jesus's story the seeds fall on four different kinds of ground.

A Hard-Packed Heart

The first is hard-packed soil. Think of a path running down the side of the field, where people have walked for years. The soil is so compact, the seeds can't penetrate the soil. They sit on top of the ground, often becoming a feast for the birds that happen by. Jesus explains, this soil is like people whose hearts are so hard to the Word of God, it never penetrates at all, and Satan snatches the Word away so that it does not have any effect in their lives. This is the *thud of a hard-packed heart.*

A Shallow Heart

A second type of soil consists of rocky ground running along the edge of the field, never properly cultivated. The soil on top is penetrable, the seeds sinking into a thin layer of dirt. The seeds sprout, but the reach of the roots is shallow, and the sun withers them. Jesus said that this is like those who are shallow in their experience of God's Word. They respond to the Word initially, but when tough times come, they fall away from commitment to God. This is *the withering of a shallow heart.*

A Congested Heart

A third kind of soil is full of weeds. Here we find seeds sown among thorny plants, and those plants choke out the good plants, causing it to be unproductive. Jesus said that this seed and soil represent those whose lives are encumbered by "the worries of this age, the deceitfulness of wealth, and the desires for other things" (Mark 4:19). These distractions choke the Word, causing it to be unfruitful in the reader's life. This represents *the languishing of a congested heart.*

A Cultivated Heart

There is a fourth kind of seed and soil. Here we have seeds falling on good ground, ground that has been well cultivated, that is receptive to the seeds and provides a context in which they can take deep root and flourish. Jesus said that this is like people who hear the Word, embrace it, and live in profound obedience to him. This is *the flourishing of a cultivated heart.*

Addressing the Condition of My Heart

If you think about it, the problem with each of these first three soils is a problem of *space.* The Word does not thrive because there is not enough room for it to thrive. Only the fourth seed and soil word picture represents a person who has a generous space—a "big" heart ready to receive and thrive in the Word of God. It is not hard, or shallow, or congested with other things that distract from the Word. There is a heart hospitality to the Word, and, more importantly, there is a heart hospitality to *the Lord of the Word*! Relationships cannot thrive without space.

In the final chapter of this book, we will discuss how to create "life space" and "heart space" for the Word of God and for the God of the Word. But for now, ask yourself which of these soils represents your life at this point in time. Examine the condition of your heart. Is there a "heart hospitality" in you? How would you diagnose your current condition? After all, if you don't deal with this issue first, you will never establish a pattern of reading the Bible well and, therefore, you will not grow as you should in your relationship with the Lord. There just won't be space for it. You have got to recognize and deal with your heart issues and make space for what matters, for ultimately, we are reading to grow in our relationship with God.

READ FOR RELATIONSHIP

My wife and I met in January of 1987. Pat was sitting on the front row of a seminary Greek class. Her professor was sick

for relationship. Later in this book we will talk about using reading plans, tools for understanding the Bible, and other helps for applying the Word of God to our lives, but we will never read well if we merely approach the Bible as a body of literature to be mastered, instead of an invitation to spend time with the Master. Remember that the Pharisees searched the Scriptures—they were deeply committed to what we call "Bible study"—but their posture toward the process was unproductive spiritually (John 5:39). They needed to come to Jesus himself for the Scriptures to speak life.

We *do* need to grow in skills, and reading the Bible well does take work at times, just as with any healthy relationship. But we need to understand that the solid bedrock for a lifetime of transformational reading is relational. Hosea 6:3 calls to us,

> Let's strive to know the LORD.
> His appearance is as sure as the dawn.
> He will come to us like the rain,
> like the spring showers that water the land.

The solid bedrock for a lifetime of
transformational reading is relational.

The term in Hebrew translated as "strive" by the CSB could be used to speak of "pursuing" something or someone, perhaps "energetically chasing after them." When I was getting to know Pat, I pursued her! I wanted a deeper relationship with her. Hosea challenges us to chase after knowing God better.

About a decade ago, our church did a biblical literacy program that I had designed called *Read the Bible for Life*. One evening, as we met in a small group to discuss our reading and reflection assignments from the previous week, it was obvious that a young mom named Jill was struggling. She was quiet, and Jill was rarely quiet. After the meeting, I asked her what was wrong. She explained that she was really struggling with reading the assigned portions of the Bible each week. Not only was she dealing with her two children, who were constantly needing attention, she simply struggled with reading. She said that she had never been a reader. So I encouraged Jill to focus on *reading for relationship*. I told her, "Don't worry about the amount that you read. Just focus on meeting God as you read. Make it about hearing from him and talking to him about the words you are reading." When she came back the next week, she was fully engaged in the discussion! Her reading of the Bible had been transformed because it had moved from a checklist assignment to a face-to-face encounter.

Later in the book we will talk about practical help in reading the Bible on a daily basis, but let me mention just two things to get you started. First, *cry out to the Holy Spirit for help.* Jesus said, "When the Spirit of truth comes, he will guide you into all the truth" (John 16:13). Ask the Spirit to lead you and speak to you in your reading. Charles Spurgeon, that great, nineteenth-century Baptist preacher, once said, "If you do not understand a book by a departed writer you are unable to ask him his meaning, but the Spirit, who inspired Holy Scripture, lives forever, and he delights to open the Word to those who seek his instruction."[3] When you start your Bible reading for the day, you can simply say, "Dear Spirit of God, please teach me as I read the Scriptures today. I want to know your Word and your will. I am ready to listen."

Second, *read rhythmically*. Choose a place and a time to meet God on a regular basis. At present, I sit in my reading chair, snugged in a comfortable corner of our gathering room, with a cup of coffee in hand, Bible and pen ready. My chosen time is first thing in the morning, when I know that other demands will rarely intrude. In an Instagram post, Leah Boden notes:

> Writer Annie Dillard said, "how we spend our days is, of course, how we spend our lives." For most, of course, that looks like work (of all varieties). But what if the real formation comes from the in-between moments; the sacred spare time; the tea break; the quiet; the closed door; the unpaid no-one is watching time. Maybe, it's our recreation and rest, how we read and relate to others, that truly marks our lives.[4]

Bible reading should be like that, a time of quiet *re-creation*, an in-between moment of sacred spare time when only One is watching. Such Bible reading *will* mark our lives.

DISCUSS

1. How might the posture of our hearts influence the way we read God's Word? How would you describe the posture God's people should take on when they read?

2. How is the Bible a lamp? A sword? A rock? Honey? Which of these characteristics do you find yourself ascribing to Scripture most often?

3. Have there been times in your life when the condition of your heart has been characterized by the different types of soils in the parable of the sower? How so?

4. What might need to change in the way you read the Bible so that you are reading for relationship?

PRACTICE

1. Spend some time asking God to make clear the condition of your heart. Ask him to move powerfully through the work

of the Holy Spirit as you read God's Word to align your heart with his will. You may pray specific passages like Psalm 71:17–22 or 119:33–40.

2. Is there sin you need to confess or reconciliation with another that needs to be sought so that you might rightly meet with God as you open his Word? A right heart is the fertile ground for fruitful fellowship with God as you read.

3. Commit to beginning your reading each day with prayer, asking God to illuminate his Word as you read so that you might better know him and obey him. Consider journaling these prayers and the passage you read so that you might see how he responds.

CHAPTER 3

Hear the Words

Dear Bibliophilos, learn to be a good listener! You cannot understand what you don't hear, and you cannot live what you don't understand.

ST. PAUL'S CATHEDRAL, BUILT by Sir Christopher Wren and consecrated in 1708, sits majestically in the heart of London, not far from the River Thames. Following the curve at the base of the cathedral's imposing dome, the so-called "Whispering Gallery" is a walkway designed for viewing the cathedral floor some one hundred feet below. Yet the gallery boasts an auditory quirk, which has made it one of the most popular accidental tourist attractions in the world. Wren did not have acoustics in mind when he built this viewing space, and yet, in a quiet moment, when background noise is at a minimum, those who have made the arduous, 257-step climb, find that a whisper spoken at any point on the wall can be heard anywhere along the wall—even on the other side of the circular walkway 108 feet away! The finely tuned acoustics, though accidental, propel a faint whisper far beyond the distance normally achieved by a softly-spoken, human voice. Such detailed crafting of St. Paul's dome has made the hearing of whispers part of a memorable cathedral experience.

HAVING "EARS TO HEAR"

Are you in a position spiritually to hear God's "still small voice" (1 Kings 19:12 KJV) "whisper" to you in the pages of Scripture? How do your "spiritual acoustics" need to be adjusted so that your Bible reading begins to "speak"? In our last chapter we saw that we need to give attention to the condition of our hearts. Jesus's parable of the seeds and the soils in Mark 4 most basically deals with that issue as foundational for reading the Bible well. As we saw, the first three soils in the parable represent hearts that don't have adequate space for the seed of God's Word to flourish in one's life. So dealing with the condition of our hearts is absolutely foundational for reading the Bible better.

Interestingly, at the end of that parable, Jesus switches from seeds to ears, saying, "Let anyone who has ears to hear listen" (Mark 4:9). Stop and think about that moment in Jesus's ministry. Obviously, he was not speaking about literal ears! It goes without saying that almost everyone in his audience had physical ears—flaps of skin and cartilage on the sides of their heads that allowed the *sounds* of his voice to register. Clearly, Jesus was not speaking about the simple act of hearing. Rather, he was speaking about *spiritual listening, hearing at another level.*

The main place that you and I cultivate skill in spiritual listening is in the pages of Scripture; it takes a particular kind of "listening," a kind of "reading attentively," for the Scriptures to become a spiritual "whispering gallery" where we can truly hear the voice of God. In his thought-provoking work *Eat This Book*, Eugene Peterson writes:

> I am interested in cultivating this kind of reading, the only kind of reading that is congruent with what is written in our

Holy Scriptures, but also with all writing that is intended to change our lives and not just stuff some information into the cells of our brain. All serious and good writing anticipates precisely this kind of reading— ruminative and leisurely, a dalliance with words in contrast to wolfing down information. But our canonical writers who wrestled God's revelation into Hebrew, Aramaic, and Greek sentences—Moses and Isaiah, Ezekiel and Jeremiah, Mark and Paul, Luke and John, Matthew and David, along with their numerous brothers and sisters, named and unnamed across the centuries—absolutely require it. They make up a school of writers employed by the Holy Spirit to give us our Holy Scriptures and keep us in touch with and responsive to reality, whether visible or invisible: God-reality. . . . They are all distinguished by a deep trust in the "power of words" (Coleridge's phrase) to bring us into the presence of God and to change our lives.[1]

"A dalliance with words." Peterson imagines a kind of reading that is more leisurely, in the best sense of the word, one that lingers over the Scriptures, with space enough for surprises, and joy, and loving confrontation by the Spirit of God.

So what practices do we need for this kind of reading to become a reality in our lives? How might we get into a "listening place" so that our ears are tuned, turning dry reading into active listening? In this chapter we consider two key practices that can help us read the words of the Bible better: reading in context and reading in a good translation.

TWO PRACTICES FOR BETTER LISTENING

Read in Context

A first, practical step to better listening to the Bible has to do with hearing the words of Scripture in context. If you think about it, context is vital for communication of any kind. Consider a stop sign. You might think that such a sign does not depend on a particular context. You read it and stop! Right?! But what if that sign is hanging upside-down in an antique shop? Do you stop when you come to *that* sign? Of course not—unless you are considering buying it. Context matters, even with a simple "text" like a stop sign.

Some contexts have to do with culture, whether the culture of a family, or a region of the country, or a whole nation. For instance, there are certain things we say in our family that you probably would not understand. You might hear me comment on an obligatory meeting I have to attend by saying, "It's oatmeal." Or during a meal someone might say, "I got *verschluckt!*" Do you understand either of these statements? If you are from a German background you probably understand the second. My wife, Pat, grew up in a German-Lutheran family in South-Central Texas, and aspects of her German heritage were passed down through the generations, including the word *verschluckt*, which is normally used when a person has had food "go down the wrong way." It is another way of saying, "I got choked!" But apart from some exposure to a German cultural context, you probably would be clueless as to its meaning.

The "oatmeal" comment refers to something that is "the right thing to do," even if you don't want to do it. We are probably the only family in the world that uses "It's oatmeal" in this way. Years ago in the US, the Quaker Oats company had a series of commercials featuring the actor Wilford Brimley. Whether he was chopping wood, or sitting at a kitchen table, or giving sage advice to a family member about the virtues of oatmeal, the commercial always ended with Brimley saying, "Quaker Oats. It's the right thing to do." One day we just spontaneously started saying, "It's oatmeal!" of things that we did not want to do but needed to do—meaning, "It's the right thing to do!" So, without an explanation from a member of our family, you probably would not understand what we meant by "oatmeal" when used in this way. To understand the statement, you need the context.

Words are funny, flexible things, if you think about it. Almost all words, including the words originally used to write the Bible, have a range of possible meanings. For instance, consider the meaning of the English word *hand* in the command, "Give him a hand!" If the statement is made by a master of ceremonies, in a small concert hall, just after a stirring piano performance, the exhortation means, "Give him a round of applause!" But if a boss says, "Give him a hand!" to an employee while pointing at another employee who is trying to lift a heavy box, you understand that he means, "Help him with that box." If the employee receiving the instruction began clapping and shouting, "Hurray!!" he might get fired!! As yet another example, if you are in a clock repair shop, and a master clocksmith says, "Give him a hand," while holding out to you the minute "hand" of a clock and nodding toward his young assistant in the next room, you understand that the exhortation means, "give him this part so that he can repair the clock." The word *hand* can also be used of a measurement for a horse, a worker on a ranch, or it can be used as a verb meaning "give"—as in, "hand him the apple."

Since words are so flexible, how do we know what a person means when they are speaking to us?! The answer is: CONTEXT!! And hearing or reading words in context *really* matters when it comes to relationships. Have you ever been quoted *out* of context in a way that was very hurtful to you? Perhaps your spouse, or a family member, or someone at work, has misunderstood you because they misread the context of a statement you made. Relational chaos can break loose in such situations. Misunderstanding a context makes for good jokes and fun romantic comedies, but in real life it can cause real problems. As I mentioned above, my wife and I communicate very well, and yet, even we have moments of misunderstanding, which have to be worked through! Often such misunderstanding stems from *misreading* what the other person is saying because we haven't understood some aspect of the context. If such misunderstanding can happen in our closest relationships, it certainly can happen when we read the Bible!

When we read God's Word, we also need to pay attention to various contexts, which can help us to read the Bible better. Since God has given us his Word in human language—he has in a sense condescended to talk "baby talk" to us, as John Calvin said—we have to "hear" God's words in context to understand them. Although his Word is divinely inspired, it still can be misunderstood by fallible, human interpreters! Since God gave us his good Word at particular times, in particular places, and in particular ways, we honor him when we pay attention to *when*, and *where*, and *how* he has communicated with us. It is a part of being a good listener. Working at understanding the contexts of Scripture is vital if we are to *hear* the words of Scripture accurately.

There are at least two broad categories of context to which we need to pay attention when reading the Bible. The first is *literary context*, and the second is *historical/cultural context*. Let me describe each, offer examples of why paying attention to that aspect of context is important, and let you know about specific tools that can help you read the Bible "in context."

Literary Context

Literary context refers to how a passage of Scripture fits and functions in the Bible. When reading a verse, or a paragraph, or a whole chapter of God's Word, we want to pay close attention to what comes before it and after it. We should ask: "Why did the author make this statement *here*?" or "Why did he say this in *this* way?"

For example, think about the very popular verse, Philippians 4:13: "I am able to do all things through him who strengthens me." We often read this passage as if Paul is speaking about extraordinary *ability*. In an American context it is commonly referred to by Christian athletes who hope in God's help as they take on an opponent. I have seen it displayed in the eye-black of a famous quarterback and on the shorts of a world-champion boxer. When I played American football in high school, we quoted this verse after we prayed together before a big game. We read the passage to mean, "I can go out there and perform well tonight (running over those other guys in the process) because God is helping me!!" Of course, players on the other team were "claiming" the same passage!! Have you ever thought of the verse when you had some monumental task to perform?

Yet, if we read the verse in its original context, it really is not dealing with ability to do great things. Take a look. Read it slowly and carefully.

> I rejoiced in the Lord greatly because once again you renewed your care for me. You were, in fact, concerned about me but lacked the opportunity to show it. I don't say this out of need, for I have learned to be content in whatever circumstances I find myself. I know how to make do with little, and I know how to make do with a lot. In any and all circumstances I have learned the secret of being content—whether well fed or hungry, whether in abundance or in need. I am able to do all things through him who strengthens me. Still, you did well by partnering with me in my hardship. (Phil. 4:10–14)

What is Paul's topic? Notice that he is talking about *contentment*, especially in dealing with resources for his ministry. Now, read the passage one more time, with that topic in mind. What is interesting is that the apostle speaks of being content whether he has a lot or a little!

Of course, there are passages in Scripture that deal with God giving us extraordinary ability when we need it. For instance, in Psalm 18:29 the psalmist shouts to God, "With you I can attack a barricade, and with my God I can leap over a wall." But Philippians 4:13 is not speaking about ability. It is speaking about contentment. It would be applicable, for instance, when we are really struggling to be content in tough times, when our resources are too little to meet the demands of the moment. Or it might be applicable when we have so much that we get nervous that we could lose what we have!

So we need to pay attention to the literary context of a passage. One thing that we can do to pay attention to literary context is simple: *slow down and read carefully*. Read what comes before your passage and what comes after it. Ask: "How does this passage 'fit' at this point in the author's argument?" We can also look at an outline of the book in a good study

Bible, or a commentary, or a Bible dictionary, identifying where the passage fits in the big picture of the book.

Let me give another example from my Bible reading this morning, one dealing with a story. Currently I am reading the gospel of John. My reading this morning was from John 11 on the "Raising of Lazarus." What a story! Read it very slowly. Notice the emotions expressed in the passage. Notice especially *Jesus's* emotions in the passage. But notice also the emotional reactions of the religious leaders. Some believed, but some thought, *Great! Now we have to kill Jesus AND Lazarus!* (John 12:10). In fact, if we look at an outline of John's gospel, we find that the raising of Lazarus comes shortly before a big turning point in the book, when the religious leaders begin to plot Jesus's death. In fact, we find that in John's gospel, it is the raising of Lazarus that prompts the religious leaders to aggressively go after Jesus in order to kill him. So the "raising of Lazarus," read in context, plays a *very* important role in the big picture of the story.

This brings me to one final point about context—the *kind* of literature we are reading in the Bible matters in terms of *how* we read. Poetry in the Psalms works differently than a letter from Paul. With poetry we look for word pictures and what they express; for a letter, the historical context often matters a great deal, for it helps us to understand why Paul or another writer is addressing the specific topics in the letter. A narrative, like the example of Jesus raising Lazarus in the previous paragraph, needs to be read in light of the main characters, the impact of actions that move the story along. We will talk about Scripture's varied literatures a bit later in the book, both how the various kinds of literature contribute to the story of Scripture and how we might learn more about reading and "hearing" them.

Historical/Cultural Context

Another type of context has to do with historical-cultural context. So what do we mean by "historical," and what do we mean by "cultural," and how does the one relate to the other? Historical context refers to historical events in the biblical era, either events recorded in the pages of Scripture or events that form the backdrop for the biblical story. Cultural context, on the other hand, has to do with attitudes, patterns of behavior, or expressions of a particular society, at a particular point in history. Both are important for reading the Bible better. I now want to give you examples of each, and at the end of the chapter I mention tools that can help you "hear" the Bible better, with more historical and cultural understanding.

For example, consider this passage depicting Jesus's words on his way to death:

> A large crowd of people followed him, including women who were mourning and lamenting him. But turning to them, Jesus said, "Daughters of Jerusalem, do not weep for me, but weep for yourselves and your children. Look, the days are coming when they will say, 'Blessed are the women without children, the wombs that never bore, and the breasts that never nursed!'" (Luke 23:27–29)

From a historical standpoint, there are two very important points of reference. First, at the time of Jesus the Roman Empire had ruled the land of Israel for about ninety years (since 63 BC). That is why Jesus had appeared before a Roman governor, Pilate, and why he was being executed in Roman fashion, by crucifixion. The Romans used crucifixion as torture, and it was considered the most shameful form of execution. In fact, normally Roman citizens could not be crucified. Part of the shame had to do with a person being *publicly humiliated*, which is why Jesus is being paraded through the streets and was to be crucified in a very public setting just outside the city. So, historically, this moment in the biblical narrative is taking place during Rome's occupation of the land. This, of course, is a huge point of reference for the *whole* New Testament. It matters in our reading of this part of the Bible.

But what about the part of the passage where Jesus says, "Look, the days are coming when they will say, 'Blessed are the women without children, the wombs that never bore, and the breasts that never nursed!'" When he mentions "the days" that "are coming," to what does he refer? Four decades after Jesus's death and resurrection, the Jewish people would rebel against Rome. In the climax of the war with the Empire, Roman forces surrounded Jerusalem, breaking through her outer walls, trapping the Jewish freedom fighters in the inner parts of the city. As those Jewish forces looked out on the hills surrounding what was left of Jerusalem, those hills were filled with crosses where captured Jewish soldiers had been crucified. Others were nailed in grotesque positions all along the walls of the outer city.

We can understand the basic *meaning* of Jesus's words in Luke 23:29 without knowing that he was speaking of a specific historical event, the fall of Jerusalem to the Romans, but we get more of the *force*, the *power* of his words if we understand a bit more of the historical background and especially what he knew was coming. What Jesus was saying, in effect, was, "I am dying on a cross today, but if you think this is bad, you haven't seen anything yet!" From Luke's *literary* context, we know that this is why Jesus wept for city, saying to the inhabitants of Jerusalem that this would happen, "because you did not recognize the time when God visited you" (Luke 19:41–44).

But what of the "cultural context" of the passage? Again, we read: "Look, the days are coming when they will say, 'Blessed are the women without children, the wombs that never bore, and the breasts that never nursed!'" (23:29). On a surface reading, this lament is understandable. If we know that Jesus is speaking of something bad that is going to happen, we may intuitively "get" that it would be a *good* thing *not* to have children or to be pregnant at such a time. But *culturally* Jesus's words are especially poignant, for in ancient Jewish culture children were considered one of God's greatest gifts. This was true in the sense of having help with work in the family; especially in agricultural situations, children were needed to help with labor. But it also was true in terms of what we think of as "insurance" or provision in old age. There were no retirement plans, no social insurance programs to take care of the aged. In one sense, if you were relatively poor (and the vast majority of people were) and had no children, you had no future. So Jesus is saying that in the future the world will be so upside-down that what is now considered the greatest blessing for a woman will seem her greatest curse.

Almost every book of the Bible has been shaped by historical and cultural dynamics. Often we can understand, on a basic level, what is going on in a passage, but it can help if we have a bit more understanding of historical context or cultural elements that shape the text. So whether we are dealing with Pharisees, or foot washing, Jesus's admonition to "go the second mile," or Paul's refusal to accept pay in Corinth, how might we get at elements of historical and cultural context? In chapter 6 we will take a look at a few tools that can help.

Read Good Translations of the Bible

A second practical step to better listening is to read the Bible in a good translation. What would you do if the words of God were *only* in the original languages of Hebrew and Greek? Well, you might learn Hebrew and Greek, but for many people that seems out of reach! Almost every person reading this chapter reads the Bible in a modern translation. The work of Bible translation is one of the most important and least appreciated of all the ministries of the modern church. In this section I want to urge you to think carefully about the *gift* of the translation you have in your hand, to understand a bit of the *process* that has gone into producing most translations, and consider how you might use various Bible translations effectively.

We Should Praise God for Translations of the Bible

First of all, the church has been using translations of the Bible from the very beginning. It may surprise you to know that the apostles Peter, Paul, and John all used a translation of the Old Testament often referred to as "the Septuagint." Most

Jews in the Mediterranean world of the first century spoke Greek as a primary language. This is because three centuries prior to the ministry of Jesus, Alexander the Great had spread the use of the Greek language throughout that part of the world, and it had become a *lingua franca*, much as English is in many parts of the world today. Consequently, for most believers of the first century, a Greek translation of the Jewish Scriptures was the translation they heard read publicly, and it was the translation most used in letters sent to the churches, some of which we have in our New Testament.

In fact, when Jesus gave what we call the "Great Commission" in Matthew 28:18–20, the words *presuppose the work of Bible translation*. Part of that passage reads: "Go, therefore, and make disciples of *all nations*." Jesus knew that the varied nations of the world would represent an amazing diversity of languages, and I think that Jesus knew that his followers would be translating the Scriptures into various languages, as a part of gospel mission. Accordingly, from the earliest centuries of the church, a part of cross-cultural and multilingual mission has been the vitally important work of Bible translation.

Second, some people have always struggled when a new translation came on the scene! If you know someone who has said, "I don't like these new-fangled translations of the Bible!" they are in good company. The great church father, Augustine, struggled with Jerome's translation of the Bible into Latin because it departed from the Greek translation used by the apostles! You may know someone who grew up with the King James translation and has the attitude, "If it was good enough for Paul, it's good enough for me!" (Of course, Paul did not use an English Bible from the seventeenth century!) But did you know that when the King James was first released it was controversial in some quarters, since it was not familiar to people? A Cambridge scholar named Dr. Hugh Broughton declared that he "had rather be rent in pieces with wild horses, than any such translation by my consent should be urged upon poor churches!"[2] He was talking about the King James Version!! In the early 1600s it was the "new-fangled" translation that was unfamiliar to most people. Yet, England's top biblical scholars of the day produced a sound, beautiful translation that would become the most popular English translation in history. It spoke the language of Shakespearean English and, thus, communicated to people of that era very well. Nevertheless, in their preface to their translation, those who worked on the King James noted that their work was just one of many good translations and that a variety of translations prove helpful for discerning the sense of Scripture. They saw the difficult work of Bible translation as one of the most important for the building up of the church.

The work of Bible translation has always been costly in terms of time, resources, and even life itself. Translators like William Tyndale *were killed for rendering the Bible in the language of common people.* There are still parts of the world today in which the work of Bible translation or the distribution of the Bible can be dangerous. But we have had brothers and sisters down through the ages who have risked life and limb in order to render the words of Scripture in the "heart language" (the language they spoke growing up) of normal people.

Third, translation work has played a vitally important part in the modern missions movement. In the 1400s, the Bible had been translated into only thirty-three languages of the world. About four hundred languages were added in the nineteenth century and another five hundred in the first half of the twentieth century. Even though modern translators continue to work to render the Bible in the various heart languages of the world, there are still over two thousand of these that have no part of the Bible in translation. Since mid-twentieth century we have seen a proliferation of English translations, and if you are an English speaker, you should be grateful—you and I have an embarrassment of riches on which to draw. So *stop right now and thank the Lord that you can read the words of the Bible in your own language.* Do not take it for granted!

What Bible Translators Try to Achieve

Bible translation work is not easy, for it demands a balance of technical skill (understanding the original languages) and artistry (rendering that language into the modern language in a way that communicates well). In fact, the best Bible translations involve a balance of three things: accuracy, clarity, and naturalness. Let me explain. *Accuracy* refers to how well a translation reflects the intended meaning and impact of the original author. Ancient words (just like modern words) often had more than one possible meaning. So translators have to grapple with which word meaning best reflects what the author intended to communicate. For example, Romans 3:23

says, "For all have sinned and fall short of the glory of God." That is a good translation. But the word we translate as *fall short* (the Greek verb *hystereō*) could also mean "lack." In fact, in the New Testament as a whole the word *normally* means "lack." If we understand "glory of God" to speak of God's active presence, as it does at points in the Bible (think of the transfiguration of Jesus, or Paul on the Damascus Road), we could understand the verse to mean that because of sin people "lack the presence of God" in their lives. That, too, is a possible translation of Romans 3:23. So, a translator grapples with questions like: "Which of these meanings is most likely given the context? Which would be the more accurate translation?"

Clarity refers to how well the translation communicates in the language of the people for whom the translation is intended. Is it clear to them? It may be accurate but not clear! For example, it would be accurate for me to translate a series of words in 1 Thessalonians 4:15 as "the Lord's *parousia*," for that is a technical term scholars use at times, which transliterates the Greek word for "coming" and speaks of Christ's Second Coming. So the translation, "We who are still alive at the Lord's *parousia* will certainly not precede those who have fallen asleep," would be accurate, but for many an English speaker on the street, it would not be clear. The translation would be much more clear if rendered as, "the Lord's coming," which is the way most modern translations have it.

Finally, *naturalness* has to do with whether a translation communicates in a way that seems "normal" to the target audience. For instance, the King James version of James 1:2 reads: "My brethren, count it all joy when ye fall into divers temptations." Now, this translation is accurate and clear—if you are a person who speaks seventeenth-century English! But it is not naturally the way a modern English speaker communicates. If fact, I have a friend from California who, as a new believer reading this verse, thought it was talking about scuba divers! He wondered what special temptations divers face! But the word *divers* in the 1600s meant "various," and that is how the Greek word is more naturally translated today. Furthermore, that word rendered *temptations* by the KJV, probably has to do with challenges in general, rather than temptations specifically (though those would be included). A more natural way of translating the verse, therefore, might be, ". . . when troubles of any kind come your way, consider it an opportunity for great joy" (NLT).

So translations try to strike a balance between accuracy, clarity, and naturalness. To achieve these goals, our major English translations have mostly been developed by teams of scholars and stylists, often working in committees. Whether you use the CSB, ESV, NIV, NLT, or some other major translation, most are good translations for which we can be grateful. But these translations have also been developed along a spectrum of those that are more "word-for-word" and those that are more "thought for thought." The New Living Translation is more thought for thought. The ESV is more on the "word-for-word" end of the spectrum, as is the New American Standard. The CSB and NIV are more in the middle, trying to balance the two approaches. But these are all good translations that seek to be faithful to God's good Word.

Let me give one point of clarification. When we say, "word-for-word" we don't mean "literal," because there is no such thing as a literal translation. *All* translations have to render the Hebrew or Greek sentences in a form that make sense in English or another target language. That process involves communicating the sense of the original language, not a rigid account giving a string of word meanings.

For example, if we try to bring the words of 1 Thessalonians 4:15, mentioned above, into English, following the Greek word order, it reads like this: "This for to you we say in a word of the Lord, that we the living the remaining unto the presence of the Lord not may precede (or attain?, or arrive) the ones having been put to sleep." Even that rendering involves interpretation of the more specific meaning of several of the Greek words involved! So, *all translations* have to interpret the words and put them in smooth English, or another language, so that they communicate to a modern reader. You and I should be thankful that there are skillful scholars and editors who are able to do so!!

Even a more "word-for-word" translation, like the ESV, has chosen, at times, to render the *thought* of the original text, rather than a rigid presentation of word meanings. For example, the New American Standard translation of 1 Corinthians 7:1 reads: "It is good for a man not to touch a woman." But the ESV (along with the CSB and NIV, for instance) translates this verse appropriately as, "It is good for a man not to have sexual relations with a woman." The problem with the NASB translation at this point is that it does not communicate accurately to a modern English speaker, since "touch a woman" normally would be heard as "have physical contact with a woman." Paul is *not* saying, "Men, have no physical contact with any woman!—do not shake hands with a woman, don't hug your daughter, etc."! Rather, in context, he clearly is talking about the advantage of singleness. Nevertheless, he immediately notes that marriage, and the sexual relationship that goes with it, is a gift from the Lord for many people (1 Cor. 7:2–7).

So there are various approaches to Bible translations, and we have many more options in English than most people in the world, who speak other languages. We are blessed to have a wealth of resources on which to draw.

How to Make Good Use of Bible Translations

Making good use of various Bible translations can help you hear the Bible better! As you think about using sound Bible translations, let me mention two things to keep in mind. First, *choose a translation that you will use most of the time for your own reading and Scripture memory.* It may be that your church has a main translation used for preaching, Scripture reading, and Bible studies, and using that translation may be a good choice for you. Over the years, use of a primary translation (and a main copy of the Bible that becomes your "go-to") can help you build familiarity with God's Word. You don't have to be rigid with this, but find a translation that you trust, one which also "speaks your language"—one that communicates to you in a natural way. The primary goal of a good translation is *communication*. So choose a translation that you can understand, and read it *a lot*.

Finally, *keep three or four translations handy for your own study and edification.* If you are an English speaker, you have lots of good translation options. Even if you have one *main* translation that you use for Bible reading, study, etc., it is a good idea to keep three or four good translations handy. This can be helpful in doing Bible study, if for nothing else except seeing where there are interpretive challenges in the passage! If three or four of the standard English translations render a verse with nuanced differences, you know that there are interpretive issues afoot and that you need to dig deeper. If you speak more than one language, you should take advantage of your skill and have a translation in each of the languages that you speak! Again, this can help you to see nuances in the biblical text and tune into interpretive issues.

Having different translations on hand also can help with Scripture memory. Above I said that you can use a main translation for your own Bible reading and Scripture memory, but there may be times when another translation captures the sense of the passage in a way that is clear to you and easier to memorize. When I use an alternative translation, I simply note that on the memory card that I am using.

I have worked on several Bible translations as a consultant, and I am passionate about the ministry of Bible translation. I often have people ask me: "Which is the best translation of the Bible?" There are two answers to that question. The first is: "On which passage?" All of the major translations have strengths and weaknesses, good renderings of the original text and better renderings of the original text. In my own Bible study through the years, I have found all of the translations mentioned above to be *good, solid* translations of the Bible, and I have found all of them to be the "best translation" on particular verses! That is why we should use a variety of translations in our own study of the Scriptures.

But the second answer to the question, "Which is the best?" is this: The best translation of the Bible is *the one that you are actually reading on a regular basis*! Again, the fact that we have good translations in our hands is a gift from God. But that gift has to be picked up and read, day in and day out, for it to have the impact on our lives that God intended in giving us his good Word. So *be thankful* for the translation that you have in hand. Don't take it for granted! And take it up and read it. Read it in context, and read it in a good translation, which will help you to hear the words of Scripture.

USE HELPFUL TOOLS TO DISCERN THE CONTEXT

First, as I have hinted earlier in this chapter, we have access to wonderful tools that can help us to read the Bible better! Make sure that you have *a good translation of the Bible*. You may want to have more than one on hand as you do your Bible reading, but have a primary translation that you use most of the time that "speaks to you," one through which the words of Scripture become familiar to you over time.

Second, buy *a good study Bible*. Study Bibles normally are produced by teams of scholars, who have poured their knowledge into copious footnotes at the bottom of each page. These notes will include words meanings, translation issues, and cross references, but they also include historical and cultural information. A good study Bible will have introductory articles on each book of the Bible, and some have articles about various points of theology or Christian living. Good study Bibles can be had for about the cost of taking your family out for a modest meal. Some of the best are the CSB Study Bible, the ESV Study Bible, the NIV Study Bible, and the NLT Study Bible. Get a study Bible *that corresponds with the translation you use the most*. Your study Bible *may* be your main reading Bible, or you might simply pick up your study Bible when you have questions in your daily Bible reading. This investment will pay rich spiritual dividends as soon as you start using it.

Third, get *a good Bible dictionary*, like the *Holman Illustrated Bible Dictionary*. Do you want to learn more about the Sadducees? The Sea of Galilee? The city of Jerusalem, the prophet Amos, or what the Bible has to say about angels? How about the historical situation behind the book of 1 Thessalonians? Or the practice of giving alms to the poor? A good Bible dictionary will also help with literary context, offering a basic outline for each book of the Bible.

By investing in a solid study Bible and a good Bible dictionary—and dipping into them regularly—you will begin to build your understanding of the Bible.

Fourth, for deeper study of historical and cultural background, you could buy a ***background commentary***. This is a special kind of commentary that focuses on historical and cultural information. Good examples include the *Zondervan Illustrated Bible Backgrounds Commentary* series, the *IVP Bible Background Commentary*, and *The Baker Illustrated Bible Background Commentary*. Each of these is filled with outstanding information on the biblical text.

DISCUSS

1. Are there phrases or inside jokes within your family or group of friends that others wouldn't understand without the context?

2. How might you begin your daily reading considering the literary, historical, and cultural context of the passage you are reading?

3. What tools do you currently use in studying God's Word? What tools do you need to work toward procuring?

4. How confident are you in using these tools today? What steps can you take toward using them better?

PRACTICE

1. Practice reading and rereading a passage, taking your time to understand and explore the text.

2. Use the questions below to establish the literary, historical, and cultural context of a passage of your choosing.

3. Complete the tools checklist and determine what you need to add to your wish list or seek out a free option for use online.

AS YOU READ FOR CONTEXT

1. Slow down and read and reread the passage.

2. Ask: Who? What? Where? When? Why?

3. Ask: What is happening before this? What happens after? What is the arc of this book of the Bible, and how does this passage or verse fit into it? What is the arc of the biblical story and how does this passage or verse fit into it?

4. What was happening at the time this was written? What was the culture like during that time and in that area? Is there a specific occasion being addressed?

TOOLS CHECKLIST

☐ A good translation of the Bible
☐ A good study Bible
☐ A good Bible dictionary
☐ A good background commentary

CHAPTER 4

Read the Rules

*Dear Bibliophilos, success in life often is
about knowing the rules and having the tools!*

I GREW UP IN a family who played various sports. My dad had
been a college basketball player, and when I was in high
school, I lettered in football, basketball, and baseball. Needless
to say, those sports were a big part of our lives. I know the
rules and strategies of those games very, very well. To this day,
when I am watching a college football game or a professional
basketball game, my mind almost automatically processes how
the teams are playing the game, where there are missteps or
violations, whether a penalty was fair, and what play a team

might do next. It is easy for me to enter into the game *because I know how the game works and its rules for engagement.*

By contrast, many of my professor colleagues are from England, South Africa, and Australia. These friends could care less if Alabama is playing Clemson for a national college football title, or whether Toronto is playing Chicago in an NBA game. Why? Because they grew up playing cricket and rugby. They *know* those games and love them, often staying up late into the night to watch their team play in a championship match. Honestly, I have watched brief snatches of a rugby game or a cricket match, but I find them really hard to watch. *I simply don't get it!* I don't know the rules, nor the strategies for how the games work, so they come across to me as not very interesting. Understanding the rules makes all the difference.

KINDS OF LITERATURE

The Bible is made up of various kinds of literature (sometimes called "genres")—for example, stories, poetry (like the Psalms), laws, biographies (like the Gospels), histories (like Acts), and letters—and each of those kinds of literature have "rules of the game" for how they can be read well. Just as trying to watch a sport or playing a board game without understanding how they "work" is frustrating, reading the Bible without understanding what we might call "the rules for reading" (guidelines for reading that part of the Bible well) can leave us disinterested and disengaged.

If you think about it, you already know a lot about different kinds of literature. You know how to "read" a cartoon. One of my favorites is *Calvin and Hobbes*. When you pick up a newspaper with a *Calvin and Hobbes* cartoon, you expect to see a little boy, who never ages and often is in trouble, a talking tiger, and a punch line that makes you laugh. You don't think it strange that there is a talking tiger in the cartoon, who very often has wise and even thought-provoking words for Calvin. Why? Because you know how cartoons work.

Similarly, you don't read a novel the same way you read a history book. My wife and I love nineteenth-century novels. But if, while we were in the middle of Jane Austen's *Pride and Prejudice*, we showed up to our weekly Bible study group and said, "Can we pray for Mr. Darcy and Eliza Bennet? They have been having problems with communication," our group members would think we were nuts, and rightly so! Novels normally don't tell us about *real* people or events. On the other hand, we read a history book to learn about real people and events, whether the golden age of the empire of Cush in Africa, or the building of the Suez Canal, or the founding of the Ming Dynasty, or the Battle of Waterloo. History and novels work differently. They have different "rules" for reading, as do poetry, and personal letters, and business letters, and menus in a restaurant. Each genre has its own purpose and its own rules for reading.

For the most part, no one sat you down and said, "Here are the rules for reading a cartoon!" You just picked it up as a normal part of your culture. If you were lucky, perhaps you had an especially good history teacher or English literature teacher along the way, who taught you how to read those kinds of literature very well. Nonetheless, you read according to the "rules" of how the various kinds of literature work in your world.

THE LITERATURES IN THE BIBLE: A FEW EXAMPLES

Yet, when we deal with the Bible, we are dealing with *ancient literature.* Some things about reading the literatures of the Bible seem intuitive to us, since we are used to reading stories, or poetry, or biographies, or letters. But, since they were written at a very different time in history and in cultures very different from our own, there are *differences* that we need to think through if we are going to read these literatures of the Bible really well. For example, if we don't know the "rules of the game" for reading Old Testament narrative or a letter written by Paul, we can feel lost, missing what God might say to us. At worst, we might become frustrated and disinterested.

Every passage you read in the Bible belongs to a particular "type" of literature, and the authors of Scripture use the various kinds of literature strategically.

Every passage you read in the Bible belongs to a particular "type" of literature, and the authors of Scripture use the various kinds of literature strategically.

As you read the Bible, you will find:

Narrative: telling a part of the Story.

Law: instructions for God's people.

Poetry: often set to song, these passages are beautifully crafted, using many literary elements like repetition, hyperbole, allegory, simile, parallelism, contrast, chiasm, and more. While many books of the Old Testament contain poetry, Psalms is only poetry and is a "hymnbook" of God's people, giving voice to praise, thanks, celebration, and lament. The Psalms can teach us how to think about God and how to process our own emotions and experiences before God.

Wisdom literature: providing wisdom and instruction for life through poetry, lament, proverbs, or stories.

Writings of the prophets: speaking on God's behalf through men he has raised up as prophets to particular people (often kings or leaders) or nations. Prophets were truth tellers, calling others to repent and turn to God. Their writings often explain current situations in a way that at times point to future happenings.

Gospels: biographies that tell the story of Jesus and proclaim the good news of the salvation he has brought.

History: recording the particular happenings of a time, specifically of the church's beginning and expansion in the book of Acts.

Letters: written to a particular person or people at a particular time, often for a particular reason or occasion.

A Sermon: prepared to be read aloud. Specifically in the book of Hebrews, this sermon's purpose is to provide a thoughtful explanation of Jesus as the fulfilment of the Old Testament.

Apocalyptic literature: often centered on a dream or vision that points to how God has broken into the world and will bring all things to his desired ends. It often uses symbolism, Old Testament imagery, and poetry (the book of Revelation and some passages within Old Testament prophets).

Each of these kinds of literature has its own "rules" for reading. Learning to read them well can help us read the Bible better. To encourage you to learn more about the Bible's genres, let me give three examples of how tuning into the kind of literature can help us read the Bible better. Here is a brief look at Old Testament stories, proverbs, and the biographies of Jesus.

Old Testament Narrative

When we read stories of the Old Testament, we need to keep a number of things in mind. First, *God is the main hero of the Old Testament stories.* It is very natural to look for a hero in the stories we read, since we probably grew up reading about heroes, whether Nancy Drew, Harry Potter, Gandalf, or Odysseus. Yet we need to get the main hero of the Old Testament stories right. God himself is always at the center of these stories, and he is working things out in amazing ways for his people. So, for instance, when we read the story of David and Goliath in 1 Samuel 17, we are not primarily reading it to understand David as a hero. The story was not written as an inspirational tale—"poor kid grows up to be king"—with the implication, "*You,* too, can be a king!" No, we should read the story of David and Goliath, first and foremost, to understand what *God* is doing in the nation of Israel at that time. He is the main character. Read that way, David is used by God to deliver his people, to bring them salvation from the Philistines.

God is the main hero of the
Old Testament stories.

Second, *the Old Testament stories have strategic tension crafted in.* This means that when we read a story from this part of the Bible, we want to ask: "What is the tension, or crisis, in this story, and why is it there?" So, for example, turn to 1 Samuel 17 in your Bible and read the story of David and Goliath again. What is the nature of the crisis? Do you see it there in the first eleven verses of the chapter? Right, the Philistines have gathered for war, and they have a champion who is the baddest of the bad! As a result, "Saul and all Israel heard these words from the Philistine" and "lost their courage." They were quaking in their sandals! The odds seemed overwhelming. They had been challenged and to lose meant that they would be slaves to the Philistines (17:9). What this tension does is set up a focus on David's faith in the God of Israel, who Goliath defied. Notice the focus on God in the passage. David tells how God had delivered him from wild animals in the past (17:34–37). David defies Goliath "in the name of the LORD of Armies, the God of the ranks of Israel" (17:45), and he confesses his confidence in God (17:46). Of course, David "overpowered the Philistine and killed him," conquering the unconquerable (17:50)! David's faith in the Living God is set over against the fear of Saul and the armies of Israel. The tension is answered with a grand conclusion.

Third, *the Old Testament stories should be read in light of God's grand Story, and we should find our place in that Story.*

We can read a story like David and Goliath to point us to one of his descendants, Jesus, who would bring salvation and rule God's people wisely, as Lord of the universe. You and I too have adversaries that defy the Living God and his people. Sin, death, the devil, and the forces of evil in the world can all seem overwhelming and tempt us to fear for our very existence. Yet, we have a champion, a King, who has defeated these enemies soundly by dying and rising for us. He now sits at the right hand of God, reigning as Lord of the universe (Phil. 2:10–11; Heb. 1:13). He says to us, "You will have suffering in this world. Be courageous! I have conquered the world" (John 16:33).

These are not all of the guidelines that we need when reading the Old Testament stories, but they will get you started. Try reading some of the narrative passages from Genesis, or 1 Samuel, or Joshua, applying these reading strategies to the stories you are encountering there. Notice the difference such an approach to reading makes in your experience of the Word of God.

Proverbs

We live at a time in history that is big on facts and "knowledge," and short on wisdom. Facts are not the same as intelligence, and intelligence is not the same as wisdom. You can have lots of facts without being smart, and you can be smart without being wise! In the Old Testament book of Proverbs, wisdom is front and center. Since, wisdom has to do with basic advice on how to live well, no book of the Bible could be more *practical*! Proverbs covers topics like, "How can I get along with my neighbor?" "How should I treat other people in my family or at work?" "How am I supposed to act when confronted with someone who is a fool?" and "How can I keep from being a fool myself!?" The short answer to our search for wisdom?: the fear of the Lord, which means to have a proper reverence and respect for God. Proverbs tells us: "The fear of the LORD is the beginning of knowledge" (1:7). We live well by living in a healthy relationship with God and then, grounded in that relationship, we live well with other people.

A key here is that *proverbs offer patterns of life and guidance, not promises*. Some proverbs *sound like* promises: "Idle hands make one poor, but diligent hands bring riches" (Prov. 10:4); "Start a youth out on his way; even when he grows old he will not depart from it" (Prov. 22:6). Those sound a lot like promises, but they were not written as ironclad assurances! Instead, they are offered to us by God as guidelines or principles for living. In essence, Proverbs 10:4 tells us that diligence in life is a sound way to live. You are more likely to be poor if you don't work. You are likely to do well if you learn how to work hard. Proverbs 22:6 encourages parents to establish good patterns of life in a child, and those patterns are likely to stick with that child throughout life.

If we read proverbs as promises, we may be disappointed. Probably many of us reading this book have worked hard in life but have not become rich. Some of us may have raised our children in church, only to see one or two of them turn away from the things of the Lord as they got older. This does not mean that these passages of Scripture have failed. Rather, life is complex. Sometimes when we do our best to follow the ways of the Lord, things do not work out as we hoped. Yet—and this is a key point—it is *always better to live according to God's ways*! These patterns of life that we find in Proverbs are always the best way to live, because they help us to live according to patterns of life that God values. They honor him.

It is always better to live
according to God's ways!

The Gospels: Biographies of Jesus

Our Gospels in the New Testament, the biographical stories of Jesus, are a bit different from what we expect in modern biographies. The latter tend to start at the beginning of a person's life and walk the reader through all the main events—birth, early years, education or lack of it, key influences and turning points, and big breaks or colossal breakdowns. Modern biographies tend to culminate in a person's legacy, whether good or bad.

The Gospels, on the other hand, don't tell us everything we would wish to know about Jesus's early years. Mark and John don't have stories about his birth or boyhood, for example, and all four Gospels focus on the short years of his ministry, especially the last weeks of his life on earth. But what they do very well is focus on the identity of Jesus and what he came to accomplish, culminating in his death and resurrection.

There are general guidelines for reading the Gospels well, some having to do with the teachings of Jesus (like how to read a parable), and others dealing with issues of cultural and historical context. We should read the structure of the Gospels as leading to Jesus's death and resurrection from the very beginning. And, especially with Matthew, Mark, and Luke, we should read the disciples as gradually coming to understand *who* Jesus really is. Reading well the miracle stories in the Gospels in this regard leads us to ask: *"What does this story tell me about Jesus?"* Let me illustrate.

In his book *Jesus Mean and Wild*, Mark Galli tells the following story about his interactions with a group of Laotian refugees who had been attending the Sacramento church where he pastored. One Sunday, these refugees, who had been attending the church for several months, approached Galli after the service, asking if they might join the congregation. Since they only had a very basic understanding of the Christian faith, the pastor suggested they go through a Bible study together on the Gospel of Mark to make sure that they understood what it means to commit one's life to Jesus. The Laotians enthusiastically agreed.

One week they studied together the passage in Mark 4:35–41, which tells about Jesus calming the storm. Under threat of life, the disciples woke Jesus up, asking him to save them. He commanded the storm to stop, and it did. Galli tells how, having read the passage, he asked the group about the storms in their lives. In response to this spiritual question, the refugees sat with puzzled looks on their faces. So, Galli elaborated, saying, "We all have storms—problems, worries, troubles, crises—and this story teaches that Jesus can give us peace in the midst of those storms. So what are your storms?" Again, this comment and question were met with puzzled silence. Finally, one of the men asked: "Do you mean that Jesus actually calmed the wind and sea in the middle of a storm?" The pastor thought that the man considered the story unbelievable, and he didn't want to get distracted with the problem of miracles. So he answered: "Yes, but we should not get hung up on the details of the miracle. We should remember that Jesus can calm the storms in our lives." Another stretch of awkward silence. Then another of the Laotians replied excitedly:, "Well, if Jesus calmed the wind and the waves, he must be a powerful man!" At this, the whole group began nodding their heads vigorously and chattered excitedly to one another in Lao. They were caught up in the *wonder* of the story! It *told them something amazing about Jesus, prompting them to ask questions about him*! With the disciples in this miracle story, they were asking, "Who then is this? Even the wind and the sea obey him!" (Mark 4:41). Great question, and it is the real point of the story.

In Psalm 107:25–30 we read as the psalmist praises the Lord God:

> He spoke and raised a stormy wind
> that stirred up the waves of the sea.
> Rising up to the sky, sinking down to the depths,
> their courage melting away in anguish . . .
> Then they cried out to the LORD in their trouble,
> and he brought them out of their distress.
> He stilled the storm to a whisper,
> and the waves of the sea were hushed.
> They rejoiced when the waves grew quiet.

Only God has the ability to calm the storm. The incredible story in Mark 4 points us toward the conclusion that Jesus is God. When we read the miracle stories of the Gospels, asking the question, "What does this tell me about Jesus?" can make all the difference.

We can't cover every type of literature in this chapter, but I hope you now see how learning about the literatures of the Bible can make your Bible reading more fruitful! To dig deeper, there are tools to help you understand the literatures more completely.

TOOLS OF THE TRADE

In our last chapter we started to explore various tools that can help us to read the Bible more effectively. Thankfully, there also are *books that deal with the kinds of literature we encounter in the Bible*. If you are just starting your journey of Bible reading, my book *Read the Bible for Life* was designed for you. Crafted as a set of interesting interviews, the book covers a wide range of topics like, "Reading the Bible as a Guide for Life," "Reading the Bible for Transformation," "Reading the Bible in Times of Sorrow and Suffering," and "Reading the Bible with the Family." But the book also has eight chapters that cover the various kinds of literature in the Bible:

Old Testament Stories

Old Testament Laws

Psalms and Proverbs

Old Testament Prophets

New Testament Stories

Teachings of Jesus

New Testament Letters

Revelation

In each chapter I interview a leading scholar and/or friend who has specialized in the topic of that chapter and offers great wisdom and practical guidance in how to read that part of Scripture well.

For a more advanced guide, which just deals with the various kinds of literature in the Bible, see the book by Gordon Fee and Douglas Stuart, *How to Read the Bible for All Its Worth*. This book is more advanced than *Read the Bible for Life* and deals with various aspects of Bible interpretation, but if you are more advanced in your Bible study skills, it may be a good resource for you.

As we read the literatures of the Bible more effectively, at least three things happen. First, we begin to *hear* the Bible more clearly. We understand what the authors were intending to accomplish through their writings, and the Scriptures begin to have a greater impact on us. Second, as we get drawn deeper into the stories of biblical narrative, or the music of the Psalms, or the wisdom of Proverbs, or the letters of the New Testament, each type of literature begins to contribute to a "symphonic" experience of Scripture—we are affected in our minds, our emotions, our imaginations, and our deepest longings. The songs of the Psalms affect us differently than the stories of the Gospels. The letters of Paul affect us differently than the imagery of Revelation. But each of these is vital for our overall experience of Scripture. And finally, these various types of literature take their places in building the overall story of Scripture. We see where the laws of the Old Testament or the teaching of Jesus in the New Testament fit in the Story. The Story begins to become much more meaningful and personally relevant to us, which is the topic of our next chapter.

DISCUSS

1. How do rules help you navigate the games of checkers or chess? Basketball or baseball?

2. What might you misread if you approach narrative as law? Or poetry as a letter? Consider how you might assume a text should be applied to your life based on its type of literature.

3. In every genre, we find the Person and character of God (Jesus in the Gospels) as central. What questions might you ask as you read to keep this in view?

4. What questions have you faced as you read God's Word in the past? What frustrations? What triumphs?

PRACTICE

1. Using the list of types of literature earlier in the chapter, write down two to three questions you might ask as you read each type.

2. Read Matthew 9:1–8. How might the details about reading Gospels earlier in this chapter help you read this passage?

3. Read Proverbs 3:1–6. Consider the instructions for reading Proverbs and discuss the wise way of living presented in this particular passage.

CHAPTER 5

Enter the Story

*Dear Bibliophilos, we all love a good story. One day,
when you wake up to find that you are in the best
Story possible, it will change your life!*

ON THE MORNING OF January 10, 1948, Marcel Sternberger boarded the subway for Brooklyn, went to his friend's house, and stayed until mid-afternoon. He then boarded a Manhattan-bound subway for his Fifth Avenue office. According to his account, as a photographer he had the peculiar habit of analyzing people's faces, and he was struck by the features of a passenger on his left. The man was probably in his late thirties, and when he glanced up, his eyes seemed to have a hurt expression in them. The man was reading a

Hungarian-language newspaper, and something prompted Marcel to say in Hungarian, "I hope you don't mind if I glance at your paper."

The man seemed surprised to be addressed in his native language, but he answered politely, "You may read it now. I'll have time later on." During the half-hour ride to town, Sternberger had a fascinating conversation with his new friend, whose name was Bela Paskin. A law student when World War II started, Paskin had been put into a German labor battalion and sent to the Ukraine. Later he was captured by the Russians and put to work burying the German dead. After the war, Paskin covered hundreds of miles on foot until he reached his home in Debrecen, a large city in eastern Hungary, only to learn that the apartments where he, his wife, and his extended family had lived were occupied by strangers. He was told that his whole family had been taken to Auschwitz; they were all dead.

Paskin was devastated; he traveled hundreds of miles across Europe and immigrated to the United States in October 1947, just three months before Sternberger met him on the subway. But Sternberger was struck by how familiar he found aspects of Paskin's story. A young woman whom he had met recently had also been from Debrecen; she had been sent to Auschwitz; from there she had been transferred to work in a German munitions factory. Her relatives had been killed in the gas chambers. Later, she was liberated by the Americans and brought to New York in 1946. Sternberger had written down her address and phone number, intending to invite her to meet his family and thus help relieve the terrible emptiness in her life. It seemed impossible that there could be any connection between these two people, but as he neared his stop on the subway he pulled out his address book and asked casually, "Was your wife's name Marya?"

Bela Paskin turned pale. "Yes!" he answered. "How did you know my wife's name?" He looked as if he were about to faint. Sternberger said, "Let's get off the train." He led Bela to a phone booth, and he stood there like a man in a trance while Sternberger dialed Marya's phone number. When she picked up the phone, Sternberger asked her where she had lived in Debrecen, and she told him the address. Asking her to hold the line, Sternberger turned to Paskin and said: "Did you and your wife live on such-and-such a street?" "Yes!" Bela exclaimed. He was white as a sheet and trembling. "Try to be calm," Sternberger urged him. "Something miraculous is about to happen to you. Here, take this telephone and talk to your wife!"

Bela Paskin nodded his head in mute bewilderment, his eyes bright with tears. He took the receiver, listened a moment to his wife's voice, then cried suddenly, "This is Bela! This is Bela!" and he began to mumble hysterically. Seeing that the poor fellow was so excited he couldn't talk coherently, Sternberger took the receiver from his shaking hands. "Stay where you are," Sternberger told Marya, who also sounded hysterical. "I am sending your husband to you. We will be there in a few minutes." Bela was crying like a baby and saying over and over again, "It is my wife. I go to my wife!"[1]

This has become one of my favorite stories. Take a moment and consider what makes this such a wonderful narrative: *Why* does it move us as it does? (Pause for a moment and jot down a few thoughts in the margin of this book.) In Sternberger's account of Bela and Marya Paskin, we have a story of tragic history turned inside-out—redeemed—the lives of two people remade. The characters and their situation draw us in, and the conclusion of the story is wonderfully satisfying—the darkest lows of human experience transformed into a life of love, joy, and hope.

THE POWER OF THE WORLD'S GREATEST STORY

If you think about it, we are *grabbed* by great stories. Stories teach us, inspire us, and delight us. They give us hope and take us to new places, while also exposing us to characters and situations that entertain us, challenge us, or shape the way that we think. Stories expand our world, helping us to imagine ways that life might be better—or could be much worse! In his essay entitled, "The Importance of Imagination for C. S. Lewis and for Us," Art Lindsley writes:

> Imagination can also lead to an expanding awareness of the world by seeing through the eyes of others. Lewis loved to read about worlds created by authors as much as he enjoyed creating his own. He loved reading novels that showed the writer's insights into life. [Lewis himself] wrote: "My own eyes are not enough for me. I will see through those of others. . . . In reading great literature I become a thousand men and yet remain myself . . ."[2]

Lewis goes on to say that a life that is never enhanced by great stories is in a sort of prison.

The fact is that God seems to have made us human beings as "story creatures." Recent research shows that stories affect our brains in ways that other forms of communication don't. For example, when you watch a bulletpoint-laden PowerPoint presentation, the Broca and Wernicke's areas of the brain get activated. These have to do with language processing by which we decode words into meaning.

When we are being told a story, however, things change dramatically. Not only are the language processing parts in our brains activated, but also *all the areas in our brains that we would use when actually experiencing the events of the story*! In other words, when we hear a story, our brains "fire on all cylinders!" When a story describes the smell of a food or the feel of a texture like leather, the sensory cortex in our brains light up. When a story tells of a character running, or a kid kicking a ball, our motor cortex lights up. When a character in a story experiences emotions, it activates the part of the brain that processes emotion. Far from an accident or quirk of nature, our love of stories seems to be hardwired into human nature. We track with stories at a deep level, and they have the power to shape our lives.

God seems to have made us human
beings as "story creatures."

Given the life-shaping power of stories, it should be no surprise that much of God's Word comes to us in the form of stories. A little less than 50 percent of the Old Testament and about 60 percent of the New Testament comes to us in story form, and the stories of Scripture fit together to form a narrative "backbone" for the whole Bible, God's "Grand Story" of how he is working out his relationship with people. That backbone gives the Scriptures a profound sense of unity.

A few years ago Chris Harrison, a professor of human and computer interaction at Carnegie Mellon University, and pastor Christoph Römhild collaborated to create a visualization of the Bible's 63,779 cross-references. They describe the graphic as follows:

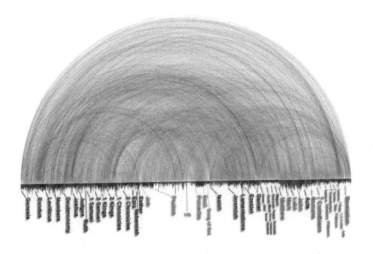

"The bar graph that runs along the bottom represents all of the chapters in the Bible. Books alternate in color between white and light gray. The length of each bar denotes the number of verses in the chapter. Each of the 63,779 cross-references found in the Bible is depicted by a single arc, creating a rainbow-like effect."[3]

This graphic captures the astounding unity and beauty of the Bible. Written over a span of more than 1,500 years, by forty or so different authors, in a variety of types of literature, the Story of God is wonderfully cohesive, all the parts knitting together in ways that are beautifully complex. As we learn the world's greatest story, we begin to see how the various parts of Scripture fit together and *why this Story matters more than any other*!

Written over a span of more than 1,500 years, by forty or so different authors, in a variety of types of literature, the Story of God is wonderfully cohesive, all the parts knitting together in ways that are beautifully complex.

AN OVERVIEW OF THE STORY

There is no greater story in the world than the story of the Bible, because no other story strikes to the very heart of our purpose as human beings—to know God himself and to have a personal, ever-deepening relationship with him. Therefore, we need to think deeply and well about the Grand Story as communicated in the Bible. As we noted above, it is a very complex story, and we don't have space in this little guide to unpack that story in detail. However, we can make a start at laying out the big picture.

One way of offering an overview for the Story is along the lines of three grand "acts," as if we had a drama on a stage unfolding before us.[4] The outline might look something like this:

Act 1: God's Plan for All People

Scene 1: Creation: The God of All of Life

Scene 2: Fall: Rejecting God's Vision for Life

Scene 3: Flood: God Judges and Makes a Covenant to Preserve Life

Act 2: God's Covenant People

Scene 1: The People: God Calls a Covenant People

Scene 2: Deliverance: God Rescues His People

Scene 3: Covenant and Law: God Embraces and Instructs His People

Scene 4: The Land: God's Place for His People

Scene 5: Kings and Prophets: God Shapes a Kingdom People

Scene 6: Kings and Prophets: God Divides the Kingdom People

Scene 7: Kings and Prophets: The Southern Kingdom as God's People

Scene 8: Exile: God Disciplines His People

Scene 9: Return: God Delivers His People Again

Act 3: God's New Covenant People

Scene 1: Christ's Coming: God's True King Arrives

Scene 2: Christ's Ministry: God's True King Manifests His Kingdom

Scene 3: Christ's Deliverance of His People: God's Work through the Death, Resurrection, and Enthronement of His King

Scene 4: Christ's Church: God's People Advance the Kingdom

Scene 5: Christ's Second Coming and Reign: God's Future for the Kingdom

Act 1: God's Plan for All People

The Story begins with *Act 1: God's Plan for All People*. In this first act we encounter creation. The title "Genesis," which designates our first book of the Bible, comes from the first Hebrew phrase in that book, *berē'shith*, which means, "in the beginning," and in the beginning there was *God*, who created the heavens and the earth (Gen. 1:1). This means that absolutely everything owes its existence to God and should be understood in light of God. He is the foundation of all that there is, and all that he made was good (Gen. 1:31).

Human beings were created in the image of God and God blessed them (Gen. 1:26–28); God gave them responsibilities and work to do and established them as part of a family (Gen. 2:8–25). It is significant that the Bible starts with Adam and Eve knowing God's presence. They walked with God in the garden (Gen. 3:8), but tragedy struck when they rebelled against God. Seduced by the serpent, they chose to discount God's words in favor of their own form of wisdom (Gen. 3:1–7). This is "the fall." Prior to the tragedy, Adam and Eve knew the presence of God in a face-to-face relationship. But they fell, turning their back on the relationship. As humanity multiplied on the earth, so did evil. So God brought judgment on the earth, destroying almost all of life with the flood (Gen. 6–9) and then scattering humanity over the earth in response to the Tower of Babylon (Gen. 11). In this first "Act" of the Story, we see that God created us as human beings, we were a part of his good creation, we face the implications and devastation of sin, and God desires to be present in our lives through relationship.

Act 2: God's Covenant People

So God has constantly reached out to humanity, working out a plan of redemption, a way of bringing people back into relationship with himself. The plan of redemption began with God creating a covenant people for himself through a man named Abram (Gen. 12:1–3). Since Abram was old and childless, God promised to make his descendants as numerous as the stars of the heavens and give them a land in which to live. Abram trusted the Lord, and that trust was credited to him as putting him in right relationship with God (Gen. 15). When he was ninety-nine years old, the Lord gave him the sign of circumcision and changed his name to Abraham, which means, "Father of a multitude," telling him that he would have a son with his wife Sarah (Gen. 17).

Abraham had a son named Isaac (Gen. 21); Isaac had Esau and Jacob (Gen. 25:19–26); and Jacob, whose name was changed to Israel (Gen. 32:28), had twelve sons who became fathers of the twelve tribes of Israel (Gen. 49:1–28). One of those sons, Joseph, was sold by his brothers into slavery in Egypt. A little more than two decades after they sold him, Joseph saved the whole family from famine, moving them to

Egypt, where they multiplied and lived for the next four hundred years (Gen. 37–50). By the end of that period, the people of Israel had become slaves of the Egyptians (Exod. 1). But, through his servant Moses, God delivered them in the Exodus by miraculous works of judgment against the Egyptians (Exod. 2–15). In the final plague against the Egyptians, the death angel "passed over" the Israelites who put the blood of a lamb on their doorposts. Thus, the Passover celebration was born (Exod. 12). In this part of the Story—especially in the almost sacrifice of Isaac and the sacrifice of the Passover lamb—we begin to see foreshadowing of the coming of Jesus.

God then led his people to the Promised Land, providing for them in the wilderness and giving them the Law of Moses as a guide and mandate for living in the land of Canaan. He also gave them instructions concerning sacrifices and worship. The tabernacle was built and the priesthood ordained (Exod. 15–40; Leviticus). But the people rebelled against God and spent forty years wandering in the Wilderness (Deuteronomy). Nevertheless, God brought his people into the Promised Land under the leadership of Joshua, and the land was divided between the tribes (Josh. 1–22). For a time, the Israelites were ruled by spiritual and military leaders called "Judges."

Their story generally follows a pattern of rebellion against God, judgment by God, deliverance by God at the hand of a Judge, and then a repeating of the cycle (the book of Judges). Eventually, not satisfied with God's leadership, the people cry out for a king to rule over them (1 Sam. 1–8).

We now go through three phases of God's people being ruled by Kings and Prophets. In the first phase, the kingdom was united and saw the rule of Kings Saul, David, and Solomon, and the leadership of a number of prophets, beginning with Samuel (1 Sam. 9–31; 2 Samuel; 1 Kings 1–11). Saul was a bad and foolish king. David, a "man after God's heart," was not only a good king but the best in the history of Israel until Christ. While David certainly had his own list of sins and errors, God promised him that one of his descendants would reign on an eternal throne (Ps. 2; 110; 2 Sam. 7). The story of David thus anticipates the coming of the Messiah. David also wrote many of the psalms. Solomon was a mixed bag, eventually giving in to his wives' idolatry (1 Kings 11), but not before he had built a temple to replace the tabernacle.

With the rise of Solomon's son, Rehoboam, the Kingdom divided into North and South (1 Kings 12). The Northern Kingdom (Israel) had all bad kings, who forsook the ways of the Lord. That kingdom was destroyed by the Assyrians in 722 BC. Prophets, including Isaiah, Amos, and Hosea, ministered to God's people during the time of the Northern Kingdom, calling them to be faithful to God's covenant.

The Southern Kingdom (Judah) had both good and bad kings but often fell into idolatry, lasting until the Exile under the Babylonians, which started in 587 BC. The Babylonians destroyed the temple built by Solomon and put an end to Israel's self-rule. In 538 BC, God delivered his people again and ended their captivity. The Persian King Cyrus allowed the Jewish people to return to their land and rebuild the temple (1 Kings 13–2 Kings; 2 Chron. 13–36). Time and again the prophets called the people of God to be faithful to the covenant with God. Finally, after the Exile, the people became focused on the Law and abandoned idolatry (Ezra; Nehemiah).

Act 3: God's New Covenant People

Four centuries later, God sent Jesus the Messiah into the world, born in Bethlehem, the town of David (Matt. 1–2; Luke 1–2). Jesus grew up in Nazareth in the home of his father and mother, Joseph and Mary. He lived a perfect life and started his public ministry at about thirty years of age (Matt. 3–4; Luke 3–4). He reconstituted the twelve tribes of Israel by calling twelve disciples, and he brought the kingdom of God, spiritually returning the people of God to his rule in their lives. Jesus carried out a ministry of teaching people how to live in his kingdom, and he did miracles that demonstrated that the power and rule of God was starting a new era of world history.

Yet, Jesus ultimately came to deal with the problem of sin and to offer people entry into a new covenant with God, one that would make possible the forgiveness needed for all people to have a relationship with holy God. Jesus died, was resurrected, and ascended, exalted to the right hand of God as Lord of all (see the Gospels). Jesus sent the Holy Spirit to live in peoples' hearts, to write the laws of God on their hearts, and to help them live for God in the world. His people became the new temple of God, the place where God dwells. They would be known as his church and sent on mission to reach the world with the good news that Jesus Christ is Lord!

The book of Acts tells about the pouring out of the Spirit on the church and the amazing first decades of the church as it spread across the Mediterranean world, proclaiming the good news about Jesus. Letters were written to the churches by

Paul and the other early church leaders, including original disciples of Jesus, like Peter and John, and the brothers of Jesus, James and Jude. The New Testament ends with the book of Revelation, which carries a message of hope for persecuted Christians in the first century but also anticipates the coming of Jesus at the end of the age.

At the heart of this Story stands the Lord God, who has always desired a people who would walk with him and know him. He is a holy God who has very particular ideas about how that must be done, but his ways are ultimately ways of life. As you and I respond to God and become part of his people—the church—we carry on this great Story embodied in the Bible.

At the heart of this Story stands the Lord God, who has always desired a people who would walk with him and know him.

EMBRACING THE STORY AS OUR OWN

We join God in the story he is continuing to write through his people, and to live it well we must know it well. Unfortunately, it is possible to have a rudimentary grasp of the Story and still not live out God's will and ways. *We must go beyond simply knowing the Story, we must embrace it as our own story!*

We join God in the story he is continuing to write through his people, and to live it well we must know it well.

One of my favorite stories is C. S. Lewis's *A Horse and His Boy*. It focuses on a young boy named Shasta, the supposed son of a crude fisherman in the land of Calorman. Shasta has a rather miserable life and has always longed to know about the mysterious lands to the North. After meeting a talking horse who tells him of the wonderful land of Narnia, Shasta runs away with the horse. On their trip north, they meet a young woman of noble birth named Aravis, who also is trying to get to the North with her friend, another talking horse. Their adventures ensue, and in an unusual turn of mix-ups, Shasta finds that he has an uncanny resemblance to the prince of Archenland, a boy named Corin, who is visiting Calorman with a delegation of Narnians. Shasta, Aravis, and the horses end up saving Archenland from invasion and realize that Shasta is really prince Corin's twin brother, Cor, kidnapped at birth. Shockingly, Cor is the true heir to the throne of Archenland.

A Horse and His Boy follows a wonderful story line. An obscure person is living out a rather mundane life, but events reveal that he really belongs in a "different story"—his true story! The boy had understood his story to be "Shasta, son of a poor fisherman," but in Narnia he learns that his true story is, "Cor, heir to the throne of Archenland." Of course, with that story comes both joys and responsibilities. But Cor embraces the story, eventually marries Aravis, and rules well over the kingdom.

What story are you living out in the world? "Bob, the bank teller"? "Jane, the primary school teacher"? "Tim, the dentist"? Those may be good and very important stories. Yet, if you are a follower of Christ, God's Word tells you that you belong in an even greater story, a story that gives deeper meaning to the other stories of your life. You are a child of the King, prince or princess of the cosmos, a participant in God's loving mission for the world, the advancement of his kingdom. That is the story of Scripture. The God of the Bible calls us into relationship with himself, so that we can know his presence, be transformed by the power of his Spirit, and live for his Son, Jesus Christ. Second Corinthians 5:15 reads: "And [Christ] died for all so that those who live should no longer live for themselves, but for the one who died for them and was raised."

I have a Jewish friend named Hanan, a lay pastor, who has spent some time touring me around Galilee in Israel. Often, when we have been talking with strangers in a restaurant or as we walked through some site of historical significance, Hanan has been asked: "Who are you and what do you do?" His response goes something like this: "I am an engineer by training, but the most interesting thing about me is that I am a follower of Yeshua (Jesus)! Are you a follower of Yeshua yet??!" Hanan presents himself as first and foremost a follower of the Lord Jesus, the One who stands at the very heart of the story of Scripture.

As we live deeply engaged with the grand story of Scripture, that greater story really does become the framework by which we understand all the other aspects of our lives. We live "for the one who died for" us. So, the question is: How might we grow in a deeper understanding and personal commitment to *that* story? Let me mention three ways to do so: immerse yourself in the Story, engage the Story in its multi-faceted power and beauty, and live with Jesus as the focus of the Story.

As we live deeply engaged with the grand story of Scripture, that greater story really does become the framework by which we understand all the other aspects of our lives.

Immerse Yourself in This Story

The most important way to learn the Bible's grand Story is by reading that story for yourself. As we read through Scripture, year after year, we gradually begin to see the broader story take shape. There are at least two ways of doing this. First, you can follow a reading plan that takes you through the Bible in *canonical order*. You probably have a Bible that is organized according to the normal order of books as they are found in the Protestant canon, beginning with Genesis, going through the books of the Old and New Testaments, ending with Revelation. There are loads of Bible reading plans, including those on the popular site YouVersion, which will offer you a daily reading plan that begins with Genesis 1 and ends with the final chapter of Revelation. These plans are laid out in lots of configurations, from a few months to three years. One reason for reading through the Bible in canonical order is that, over time, you become more and more familiar with the location of various passages in Scripture. The challenge can be that the normal canonical order of books in our Bibles does not correspond to the chronological order of events in biblical history, so we don't get a sense of how all of the biblical materials fit together in *one* Story.

This brings us to a second option for immersing yourself in the Story: use a *chronological Bible or reading plan to read through the Bible*. There are Bibles and Bible reading plans that have been formatted in a way to take a reader step-by-step through the story of Scripture. My *CSB Day-by-Day Chronological Bible*, published by Holman Publishers, is one example, and it includes daily "coaching" on how to read the portion for each day. You receive tips for reading the kind of literature encountered in the passage, as well as insights into how the passage fits into the grand story of Scripture. *The One Year Chronological Bible* produced by Tyndale Publishers is another example of a popular, chronological Bible. If you want to use your own Bible and translation to read through the Story chronologically, my *Reader's Guide to the Bible* is laid out as a one-year reading plan that also includes the daily coaching mentioned above, and there are other chronological plans found on the YouVersion site (youversion.com).

As You Read, Ask "Story" Questions

To really embrace the Story, you need to understand the Story, and to understand the Story, you need to ask good questions about what you are reading. Story-type questions will, of course, work best with narrative material, but even as we deal with laws, or psalms, or the prophets, we can still ask questions like, "When did this take place and why?" or "Who is involved in this part of the Bible's story?"

Here are a few questions to ask as you work your way through the story of Scripture:

Who are the main characters?

How are their lives different from ours?/How do their lives parallel our own?

Are there obvious protagonists (the good guys) and antagonists?

What is being introduced in the story?

Is there a "cause" and "effect" element to the events described?

What is the main tension or crisis?

How does the tension or crisis get resolved?

When and where do these events take place?

What does this passage tell me about God, people, or a right relationship with God or others in the world?

How might I work the truths here into my life this week?

As you probe the text with these questions, read the passage through slowly and carefully. When you hit a question that you cannot answer, utilize tools like a study Bible or Bible dictionary. Jot down notes in a journal, a notebook, or the margins of your Bible. Through the years such notes become "friends" that "speak" to you over and over again. The main point here is to read the Bible *actively*, asking questions of it as you open your heart and life to its pages!

Read the Bible *actively*, asking questions of it
as you open your heart and life to its pages!

Live with Jesus as the Focus of the Story

Finally, there is no greater way to grow in your own engagement of the story of Scripture than to see Jesus as the focus of the Story. All of the Old Testament builds to a climax in Jesus, his life and ministry, his death, resurrection, and exaltation, and all of the New Testament flows from his identity and work in bringing us into new covenant relationship with the Father.

Earlier, I mentioned that there is much in the Old Testament that anticipates the coming and ministry of Jesus, our Messiah. Whether we are dealing with Moses as a leader of God's people, the Passover lamb that was slain so that God's people would not die, the sacrificial system of the Old Testament, the priesthood of the Old Testament, David as God's king and the Messiah's ancestor, the Suffering Servant of Isaiah 53, and so, so, so much more, we find that the Old Testament lays an amazing foundation for the life, ministry, and work of Jesus! The author of Hebrews says it this way:

> Long ago God spoke to our ancestors by the
> prophets at different times and in different
> ways. In these last days, he has spoken to us
> by his Son. (Heb. 1:1–2)

The translation sounds sequential: "God did *this*. Then God did *that*." The original Greek text makes clearer the relationship between the older revelation (the Old Testament) and the newer revelation brought through Jesus. It reads: "God, *having* spoken . . . , spoke!" The term translated as "having spoken" (a participle) depends on the main verb as a point of reference. What this means is the Old Testament Scriptures are connected to, prepare for, and culminate in the revelation that was brought through Jesus, God's Son. *Having spoken* in the Old Testament era, God *spoke* to us through his Son. This corresponds to the fact that the New Testament Gospels focus a great deal on Jesus's life and ministry as a fulfilment of the Scriptures.

The rest of the New Testament draws out the implications of that reality for those who are followers of Jesus. Jesus, God's Son, who came to earth to live as a human being, was crucified for the forgiveness of our sins. He died, was buried, resurrected, and exalted as Lord of the universe to the right hand of the Father. His followers traveled the world, proclaimed the gospel, and planted and supported churches throughout the Mediterranean world. Each book of the New Testament teaches followers of the Lord Jesus how to think well and live well for him. In him, all the parts of the Bible fit together and make sense. Jesus is the key.

So reading the Bible and grasping the grand Story should drive our commitment to Jesus as Lord and our learning to live like him as deeply committed followers. This Story leads us to shape our individual stories in light of the call, claims, commands, and commission of Christ himself, viewing even our most everyday moments as opportunities to obey him and make him known. This is why Dr. Emily Walker Heady notes:

> If we ignore the story-like elements of the biblical narrative, we miss the fullest potential of its work in our lives. The Gospel is not a factory, making useful and uniform disciples from a supply of raw souls. It works on us as a plot works on its characters, inviting us to come and help shape the story.[5]

Similarly, Will Herberg writes:

> Redemptive history is not merely a recital that we hear and understand. It is also a demand upon us, for out of it comes the voice of God. Faith is responding to the call

of God . . . [when we read the Bible] it is as though we sat witnessing some tremendous epic drama being performed on a vast stage, when suddenly the chief character, who is also its director, steps forward to the front of the stage, fixes his eye upon us, points his finger at us and calls out: "You, you're wanted. Come up here. Take your part!"[6]

As we grow in understanding the big picture of the biblical story, we will understand our "part" better and the wonderful privilege of living out the greatest story of all time!

DISCUSS

1. When in your life have you been completely captivated by a story? (Consider movies, podcast series, television shows, theatre, and so forth.) Why did that story speak to you?

2. Which "Act" of Scripture's grand story do you find yourself most drawn to? What holes might you have in your own

understanding of the whole story of Scripture? How might you seek to fill in any gaps?

3. What story would others see you as living out in the world? Do people know you more by your vocation or by how you seek to live your life for Jesus?

4. What might it practically look like to enter into the story of Scripture deeply? Who do you know who does this well? Describe how their life is marked by the story of Scripture.

PRACTICE

1. Practice telling the story from Genesis to Revelation in three minutes or less. What are the key themes to include? The most important moments?

2. What is your strategy for reading the Bible? Are you reading canonically? Chronologically? If you haven't chosen a strategy, commit to one today.

3. Turn to Genesis 37, a very familiar passage. Practice asking the questions found in the section titled "As You Read, Ask 'Story' Questions."

CHAPTER 6

Pack Well

Dear Bibliophilos, life is a journey. Pack well!

I HAVE JUST FINISHED rereading one of my favorite books, J. R. R. Tolkien's *The Hobbit*, a delightful tale of how the wizard Gandalf enlists Bilbo Baggins, a quiet and unassuming hobbit, to go on a treasure-hunting adventure with a bunch of dwarves. A key moment in the story comes when Bilbo has to decide whether he will embrace the adventure. He has overslept and must rush immediately to a rendezvous point if he is to meet the dwarves in time to go with them into the wilds of the world. He is unprepared.

To the end of his days Bilbo could never remember how he found himself outside, without a hat, a walking stick or any money, or anything that he usually took when he went out; leaving his second breakfast half-finished and quite unwashed-up, pushing his keys into Gandalf's hands, and running as fast as his furry feet could carry him down the lane, past the great Mill, across The Water, and then on for a mile or more.

Very puffed he was, when he got to Bywater just on the stroke of eleven, and found that he had come without a pocket-handkerchief![1]

But go he does—unprepared! By the end of the story, which involves trolls, goblins, elves, a shape-shifter named Beorn, and a great and terrible dragon, the little hobbit has had the adventure of a lifetime and become a hero in the bargain—even though he went quite unprepared.

In real life, journeys normally take a bit more planning and packing. As I write this book, my wife Pat and I are living in Cambridge, England for a five-month research leave from the college where I teach. Too soon it will be time for us to go home, and when the time comes, we are going to need to make decisions about what to pack. You see, my wife loves both dishes and books—especially big, bulky cookbooks! And both books and beautiful, English dishes are wonderfully inexpensive at British "charity shops" (what we normally call "thrift stores" in North America). But decision day for our collection is coming! Airlines have limits on luggage! We are going to have to decide what needs to be taken with us and what we will leave behind.

Like Bilbo, you have been invited, through the pages of this book, on an adventure, a quest to learn how to read the Bible better. You may feel woefully unprepared, but into the adventure of God's Word you must go. Yet, unlike Bilbo, you can use some of the pages of this book to aid you in your packing. What will you take with you once you set this guide aside? As you take up your Bible to read in the weeks and months ahead, I would like to suggest that you pack a number of things for the journey: good tools, a pair of walking shoes, and wonderful companions.

PACKING FOR THE JOURNEY

Good Tools

As we have worked our way through this book, I have mentioned briefly that there are tools to help us read the Bible better. At this point I want to remind you of some of those tools that will help you engage in productive Bible reading for the rest of your life. So write these down, and invest in them right away! Whether you are dealing with issues of literary context, looking for information concerning some aspect of the historical or cultural background of the Bible, or you want to dive deeper into a particular passage of Scripture, these tools can help. Let me begin with the three most basic, affordable tools that can help you right away with your Bible reading. They are easy to use and immediately will make a big difference in your Bible reading.

We discussed a number of tools in chapters 3, 4, and 5. Let's take a moment to review those and add one final tool to the list.

1. *A good translation of the Bible.* If your primary language is English, there are a

number of sound options, like the CSB, ESV, NIV, or NLT.

2. *A good study Bible.* Some of the best are the *CSB Study Bible*, the *ESV Study Bible*, the *NIV Study Bible*, and the *NLT Study Bible*. Get one *that corresponds with the translation you use the most*. It *may* be your main reading Bible, or you might simply pick up your study Bible when you have questions in your daily Bible reading. This investment will pay rich spiritual dividends as soon as you start using it.

3. *A good Bible dictionary*, like the *Holman Illustrated Bible Dictionary*. Do you want to learn more about the Sadducees? The Sea of Galilee? The city of Jerusalem, the prophet Amos, or what the Bible has to say about angels? A good Bible dictionary will help with such topics, but it also can help with a book's

literary context, offering a basic outline for each book of the Bible.

4. ***A background commentary.*** This is a special kind of commentary that focuses on historical and cultural information. Good examples include the *Zondervan Illustrated Bible Backgrounds Commentary* series, the *IVP Bible Background Commentary*, and *The Baker Illustrated Bible Background Commentary*. Each of these is filled with outstanding information on the biblical text.

5. ***A guide for reading particular types of biblical literature.*** As noted in chapter 4, if you are just starting your journey of Bible reading, my book *Read the Bible for Life* may be beneficial for you. For a more advanced guide, see the book by Gordon Fee and Douglas Stuart, *How to Read the Bible for All Its Worth*.

6. ***A chronological Bible or a good reading plan.*** As we discussed at the end

of chapter 5, a chronological Bible or reading plan can help you establish the habit of daily Bible reading and give you a sense of the framework of the story of the Bible.

7. *A good commentary.* This is a tool that we have not addressed yet, but as you grow in Bible reading, a good commentary can help you dig deeper into the Scripture. Whereas a "background commentary" focuses on historical and cultural contexts, most commentaries on a particular book of the Bible will deal with a wide range of issues to help in understanding particular passages in that book. Specifically, when your Bible Study group, pastor, or Sunday school class is studying through a specific book of the Bible, consider getting a good commentary on that book. There are lots to choose from, and they cover a wide range of levels, but

five series from which you might draw are the *Christian Standard Commentary*, the *NIV Application Commentary*, the *Tyndale Old Testament Commentary* and *New Testament Commentary* series, and the *ESV Expository Commentary* series.

So here is a checklist of tools to consider buying as you start your journey:

Top Priority

☐ a good translation of the Bible

☐ Bible reading plan/chronological Bible

☐ a good study Bible

Other Important Tools

☐ a good Bible dictionary

☐ commentaries/a background commentary

☐ a book on understanding the kinds of literatures in the Bible

Walking Shoes

Second, we need "walking shoes." As Pat and I prepared for our extended stay in England this fall, we did a good deal of research on shoes that were good for walking in all kinds of weather. When we are in England, we don't have a car, and we walk just about everywhere. So, I knew that getting a good pair of shoes that would hold up, even in the rain, would be important. I bought a pair that have worked out really well, and its a good thing! My phone tells me that in the past four months I have walked a total of about 350 miles! How did that happen? Pat and I hit the streets, walking almost everyday to get groceries, or run errands, or just to take a stroll through town. On weekends we often went for longer hikes, through the meadows leading to the village of Grantchester, or for an outing to charity shops on Mill Road in Cambridge. We built up "walking legs" by walking consistently. The miles added up without us even thinking about it.

Nothing in this book will help you in reading the Bible, *unless you walk the walk, building a habit of reading the Bible on a regular basis.* You and I have got to make a conscious decision to embrace Bible reading as a normal, rhythmic aspect of our daily lives. As we noted in our chapter, "Look to the Heart," to do this, we need to work "life space" and "heart space" into our lives.

You and I have got to make a conscious
decision to embrace Bible reading as a
normal, rhythmic aspect of our daily lives.

Life Space

What I mean by "life space" has to do with our daily schedules. As I mentioned at the end of chapter 2, I want to suggest that you choose a specific time and a specific place to have your time of Bible reading each day. I do my Bible reading in the morning, with a cup of tea or coffee in hand in a special place. The rhythm is as natural as breathing, and I can't imagine missing that time regularly. In fact, I long for it like I long for a meal when I am hungry. You may find that lunchtime, or a time in early evening works best for you, but I find that morning is best for me since it avoids distractions or fatigue from a busy schedule.

Begin by reading for about 15 minutes per day. Believe it or not, with that basic commitment, you can read through the Bible in less than two years! Move that time up to 25–30 minutes a day, and most people can read through the Bible in a year. So set apart the time so you won't be rushed, and read with a pen in hand, ready to underline parts of the Bible that speak to you. You may also want to buy a journal to jot down notes, insights, or questions that come up during your Bible reading.

Such practices will help you build "life space" for a regular engagement of the Bible. The rhythms of a place and time and pattern of reading and engaging the Scriptures can build "walking legs" over time and you will find it amazing how far you can go spiritually.

Heart Space

Along with life space we also need to build "heart space." When we read the Bible, we need to do much more than simply gather *information*. We need to read for *transformation*!

That means that we are going to need to have hearts that are open to living the words that we are reading. In other words, we need to apply Scripture to our lives in ways that matter in the nitty-gritty of everyday life. There is *nothing* that will transform your own reading of the Bible and draw you into the story of Scripture like applying its truths to your own life. As you see Scripture transforming you, you will begin to understand aspects of the Story in new ways.

When we read the Bible, we need to do much more than simply gather information. We need to read for transformation!

Earlier we emphasized the importance of a heart that is receptive to God's Word, one that is "cultivated," like good ground ready to receive a planted seed. Let me shift the word picture a bit. When our kids were small, my wife trained them to think about the condition of their heart in relating to us, to each other, and to the Lord. Especially if they were having a bad attitude and were not opening up to us, Pat would hold a piece of Play-Doh in one hand and a rock in the other. She asked Joshua or Anna: "Is your heart soft right now, like this Play-Doh, or is it hard like this rock?" The illustration helped them learn to "soften" their hearts, a lesson that all of us need to learn continually in our spiritual lives. Application of God's Word will come more naturally to us if we have soft hearts toward God, hearts that long to please him in all that we do. As you start your Bible reading each day, ask the Holy Spirit to guide you in your reading and speak to you on matters that need to be addressed in your life. This is making "heart space" for God's Word.

Companions

On our journey to reading the Bible better, we not only need good tools and "walking shoes," we need other people with whom to walk. Not long ago, a half marathon was run in the city where I currently live, and I noticed something interesting. There were top athletes running in the race, of course, but there also were "normal" people, people of all backgrounds and ages and levels of ability. Often these normal people, some of whom did not look very athletic at all, ran or walked in groups. I saw one group of older ladies, none of whom seemed in top shape, walking together in their running shoes and colorful outfits, almost walking arm in arm as they made their way to the finish line. They looked like they *needed each other* and *enjoyed each other* during the race.

As we think about building a life of reading God's Word really well, we, too, need others in the body of Christ to walk with us. We simply cannot sustain a life of reading, understanding, discussing, and living the Bible apart from other Christ-followers. In his book *Christ Plays in Ten Thousand Places*, Eugene Peterson writes: "There can be no maturity in the spiritual life, no obedience in following Jesus, no wholeness in the Christian life, apart from an immersion in, and embrace of, community. I am not myself by myself."[2] Reading the Bible in and with a community will help us to read the Bible better.

So here are a few things to consider as you begin to read your Bible. First, *read with a friend or friends.* As you start your own process of Bible reading, invite others to read with you. You might plan to read through the Bible together over the next year or two, or you could choose a book of the Bible like the gospel of John to read through together. You could invite your friend(s) to meet with you on a regular basis to *read aloud* together, or each of you could read the Bible on your own time but then come together to discuss what you are reading. These fellow readers may be members of your own family (you could even have a family devotion time every day), a friend from church, or some other person or persons from your broader community. But read and discuss the Bible with others. Their companionship will encourage you, their insights will stimulate your thinking, and their presence will keep you on track in your reading process.

Second, *be a good listener.* As you hear the Word read or taught or preached in church, train yourself to be an attentive, engaged listener. Take notes. Think about what you are hearing, packing away high-impact insights in the corners of your heart to consider more deeply later. Memorize key passages that stick out to you as especially significant for your own life and journey, meditating, "listening internally," over and over again to a passage until it becomes a part of you. And when your friend(s) share with you about the things that the Lord has been teaching them in the Word, *tune in.* Live out a ministry of *listening* and *encouraging* those around you.

Live out a ministry of listening and encouraging those around you.

Finally, *be generous, giving of your own time and resources to promote Bible reading in your community*. You and I value that in which we invest personally. Most Bible study groups, churches, and other forms of Christian community need people to lead, serve, or support their ministry in some way. You may have gifts of teaching, leading, service, or giving that can be put to use in *building a community of Bible reading and Bible living*. Your very presence will help encourage others in their own commitments to the Word. How might the Lord use you and your gifts to promote Bible reading in your context? Malcolm Guite, in his poem titled, "As If," challenges us to be givers in our communities.

> The Giver of all gifts asks me to give!
> The Fountain from which every good thing flows,
> The Life who spends himself that all might live,
> The Root whence every bud and blossom grows,

Calls me, as if I knew no limitation,
As if I focused all his hidden force,
To be creative with his new creation,
To find my flow in him, my living source,
To live as if I had no fear of losing,
To spend as if I had no need to earn,
To turn my cheek as if it felt no bruising,
To lend as if I needed no return,
As if my debts and sins were all forgiven,
As if I too could body forth his Heaven.[3]

Giving is not easy for some of us. But such a pattern of life pays rich dividends. As you give generously of your time and efforts to build a community of Bible readers, you will find your own love for and commitment to God's Word growing, and that will have a profound impact in the world.

DISCUSS

1. Have you ever traveled to a destination without the correct items packed? Or has an airline lost your luggage and left you without anything you packed? How did you respond?

2. What tools do you currently use in your study of the Bible? Which tool will you seek to get next?

3. Are you consistent in your Bible reading now? Why or why not?

4. How might you cultivate more life and heart space in your life? How might you seek to share God's good Word with others in your community?

PRACTICE

1. As you seek to be more consistent in your Bible reading, choose a time and place you will meet with God everyday. Tell a friend and set an alarm!

2. Read for fifteen minutes today and record any insights in a journal or note on your phone. Throughout the day, consider the ways God might use what you read to encourage you or others.

3. God is in the business of changing lives through his Word. What rhythms will you commit to following this week? This month? This year? How will you share what God is doing with others?

4. How has this book changed the way you approach God's Word? What have been the insights that have affected you most?

A Final Note to the Reader

DEAR READER, WELL DONE on taking first steps to reading the Bible better. The journey on which you are embarking will demand effort, but it is so worth it! This wonderful gift, God's good Word, has been given to us as a foundation on which to build life, as a guide by which to live life, and as an encouragement by which to sustain a lifelong commitment to Christ and his Church. Here is help. Here is hope. And here is power! Never underestimate the power of God's good Word. As you commit to reading the Bible better, it can become transformative for your life and for the lives of those around you.

In 1999 Rosaria Butterfield had been serving as a tenured professor of English at Syracuse University. She specialized in gay studies at the university and had been living in a lesbian relationship for about ten years. Yet in her book, *The Secret Thoughts of an Unlikely Convert*, she tells of two powerful forces in her life, which eventually brought her to the feet of Jesus Christ as her Lord. First, local pastor Ken Smith and his wife reached out to Rosaria, inviting her to dinner. Over the next two years the Smiths loved her and her friends consistently and sacrificially. They got to know her, answered her questions, and embraced her as a friend. They provided a relational context in which Rosaria could see the reality of the Christian life embodied in sincere followers of Christ.

Second, she began to read the Bible. Not long ago, in a blog interview, Rosaria was asked how something as simple as repeated and voracious Bible reading had changed her. How did her engagement with the Scriptures change an intellectual, postmodernist, activist, university professor to someone who loved Christ and was willing to spend the balance of her life in following him? She commented:

> At first, ideas like the Bible's inerrancy, infal-
> libility, sufficiency, and authority seemed
> outrageous, insulting and ridiculous. But
> after reading the Bible in big chunks, five
> hours at one sitting, many days in a row, I
> could see how, if only I loved the things that

God loved, these ideas could become the bridge to what the Bible calls the fruit of the Spirit. I was a divided woman, and the Bible is what tore me in half. I felt pitted between not wanting to repent of my sin (and not really knowing how one repents of a sin of identity) and deeply wanting Jesus, the Jesus who promised a yoke easier than the one that bound me and a burden lighter than the one that crushed me. Finally, when the Bible got to be bigger inside me than I, I realized that the Bible is the only book in the world that is alive. . . . The Bible compelled me, drew me in, revealed to me that the threshold to God is repentance. It convinced me that the only way to save my life is to lose it. And at the same time, I saw how the Bible organized not just a "me and Jesus" sort of life, but a Bible-believing community.[1]

The living Word of God confronted Rosaria Butterfield, compelling her, drawing her. God met her in the pages of

Scripture and changed her, and he did it in the context of community.

God wants to do the same in each of us. You and I, and our communities of Christ-followers in which we live, are called to "come and hear," to walk with the God of grace and truth and joy as he speaks to us in the pages of Scripture. So, dear friend, as you have read this short guide about words, I hope that it has helped you. My prayer is that, as a result, you will read the Bible better, and in reading it better, you will read it consistently, and in reading it consistently, you will live it out all the days of your life, to the good of Christ's Church and to the glory of God.

Notes

Chapter 1

1. The name *Bibliophilos* means, "Friend of the Book." If that designation fits you, I will thus address you at the beginning of each chapter of this little guide.

2. Levi Lusko, *I Declare War: Four Keys to Winning the Battle with Yourself* (Nashville: Thomas Nelson, 2018), 81.

3. From Nathaniel Hawthorne's "Note-Books" (Part XII), published in *The Atlantic*, December 1866.

4. A paraphrase of Ecclesiastes 10:10a.

Chapter 2

1. Harold W. Attridge, *Hebrews: A Commentary on the Epistle to the Hebrews, (Hermeneia: A Critical and Historical Commentary on the Bible)* (Philadelphia: Fortress Press, 1989), 133.

2. J. R. R. Tolkien, *The Lord of the Rings, Part Three: Return of the King* (1955; repr., New York: Random House, 2018), 211.

3. Charles H. Spurgeon, *Commenting and Commentaries: Lectures* (New York: Sheldon and Company, 1876), 58.

4. Leah Boden, Instagram post, March 21, 2021, https://www.insta gram.com/p/CMrDfzAB2xs/?igshid=g0jn0wdxmbj0.

Chapter 3

1. Eugene Peterson, *Eat This Book* (Grand Rapids: Wm. B. Eerdmans, 2006), 3.

2. As quoted in Paul D. Wegner, *The Journey from Texts to Translations* (Grand Rapids: Baker Academic, 1999), 313.

Chapter 5

1. Paul Deutschman, *Great Stories Remembered*, edited and compiled by Joe L. Wheeler (Colorado Springs: Focus on the Family Publishers, 1996).

2. Art Lindsley, "The Importance of Imagination for C. S. Lewis and for Us," *Knowing and Doing: A Teaching Quarterly for Discipleship of Heart and Mind* (Summer 2001): 3, https://www.cslewisinstitute.org /webfm_send/277.

3. Graphic taken from https://churchm.ag/wp-content/uploads /2013/09/Bible-Cross-References-Infographic.jpg; used by permission.

4. This is the approach taken in my *Day-by-Day Chronological Bible* (Nashville: Holman Bible Publishers, 2018) and the *Reader's Guide to the Bible: A Chronological Reading Plan* (Nashville: LifeWay Press, 2011).

5. Quote taken from a B&H Academic Blog that is no longer live entitled "What Good Are Stories?", published on March 3, 2015. Used by permission.

6. Will Herberg, "Biblical Faith as *Heilsgeschichte*: The Meaning of Redemptive History in Human Existence," *The Christian Scholar* 39, no. 1 (1956): 25–31.

Chapter 6

1. J. R. R., Tolkien, *The Hobbit* (1966; repr., New York: Random House, 1982), 30.

2. Eugene Peterson, *Christ Plays in Ten Thousand Places: A Conversation in Spiritual Theology* (Grand Rapids: Wm. B. Eerdmans, 2005), 226.

3. To hear Malcolm Guite recite his poem "As If," see https://www.theworkofthepeople.com/as-if.

A Final Note to the Reader

1. Joshua Rogers, "Five Questions with an Unlikely Convert," Boundless, July 13, 2015, https://www.boundless.org/blog/five-questions-with-an-unlikely-convert/.

Develop a habit
of reading the Bible
◇━━━━━ everyday ━━━━━◇

CHRISTIAN
STANDARD
BIBLE®

Day ◆ Day
Chronological
Bible

with Daily Readings
Guided by
Dr. George Guthrie

FAITHFUL ≡ TRUE ▸

━━━ available where books are sold ━━━

CONTINUE
LEARNING

available where books are sold